Quilt Block Fusion

Combining Innovative Piecing Techniques
to Create Perfect Blocks with Ease

Landauer Publishing, LLC

Quilt Block Fusion

Combining Innovative Piecing Techniques
to Create Perfect Blocks with Ease

Copyright© 2013 by Landauer Publishing, LLC
Projects Copyright© 2012 by Penny Haren

This book was designed, produced,
and published by Landauer Publishing, LLC
3100 101st Street, Urbandale, IA 50322
515-287-2144; 800-557-2144; landauerpub.com

President/Publisher: Jeramy Lanigan Landauer
Vice President of Sales & Administration: Kitty Jacobson
Editor: Jeri Simon
Art Director: Laurel Albright
Photography: Sue Voegtlin

Library of Congress Control Number: 2013933180
ISBN 13: 978-1-935726-33-3

This book is printed on acid-free paper.
Printed in United States
10 9 8 7 6 5 4 3 2 1

For more than 30 years as a quilter, and several years as a quilt shop owner, Ohio-based Penny Haren has been developing and teaching techniques that make it quick, easy and fun for quilters of all skill levels to create intricate blocks with stunning results. Her technique, Penny Haren's Pieced Appliqué®, eliminates inset points and curves from even the most complicated blocks. Quilts and blocks that you might never have considered are now not only possible but a breeze. Penny introduced her innovative pieced appliqué technique at Spring Quilt Market 2008 in Portland, Oregon.

Her latest "stroke of genius" technique combines pieced appliqué with paper-piecing. This book, Quilt Block Fusion, builds on the paper-pieced appliqué techniques as well as new and innovative ways to construct classic blocks such as dresden plates and baskets.

Penny also designs rulers for Creative Grids®. These rulers help save time, make quilting even easier and add the "ahhh" factor to all your projects. Along with the rulers, she has developed a line of quality notions available through independent quilt shops.

In her "spare time", Penny consults with and writes the newsletter for Checker Distributors®, the most diverse distributor of books, patterns, notions and fabrics serving the independent quilting, sewing and needle arts retailer worldwide. She also writes a notions column for FabShop News – a bi-monthly publication for shop owners.

On the home front, Penny is a mother of four sons, one daughter, and two "bonus" daughters. She is also the proud grandmother of five.

Since the introduction of pieced appliqué, Penny has been in demand for teaching and workshops around the country. She promises, "If you are like the thousands of women I have taught, you may never look at a block pattern the same way again."

If you would like Penny to teach at your shop or guild, contact her at pennyharen70@hotmail.com.

Penny

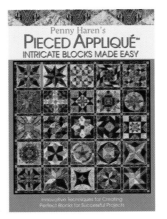

Find more books by Penny Haren at your local quilt shop, favorite book seller or visit landauerpub.com

Table of Contents

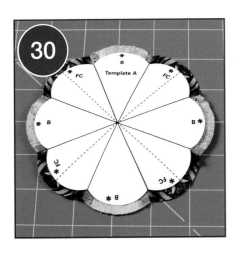

Rambler

Central Park

Pointed Dresden Plate

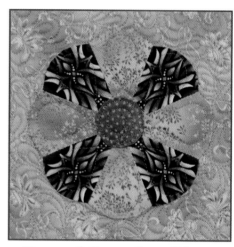

Round Dresden Plate

Grandmother's
Flower Garden

Basket

Learn 10 techniques

Basic Paper-Piecing

Paper-Pieced Appliqué

Paper-Piecing with Fussy-Cut Segments

Paper-Piecing with Pieced Segments

Paper-Piecing with Flipped Back Appliqué

Strip-Pieced Appliqués

Pointed Dresden Plate

Round Dresden Plate

Strip-Pieced Grandmother's Flower Garden

Machine-Pieced Grandmother's Flower Garden

Learn all the techniques by following the easy, step-by-step photographs and instructions found throughout the General Instructions, beginning on page 10, and the Technique Notebooks, beginning on page 24.

All the blocks created can be used in any of the projects beginning on page 55.

Watch Penny demonstrate her techniques at
landauerpub.com/Quilt-Block-Fusion-Penny-Haren.html

Projects

Grandma Emma's Garden Quilt

Sydney's Quilt

Basket Table Topper

Introducing Paper-Pieced Appliqué

Paper-pieced appliqué combines paper-piecing and pieced appliqué to create accurate and intricate blocks quickly and easily. All the techniques needed to create these paper-pieced appliqué blocks are clearly shown so even beginners will be successful.

With Paper-Pieced Appliqué you can

- Position appliqué points and curves on a traditional paper-pieced block to create intricate blocks without difficult machine piecing.

- Eliminate the frustration of piecing inset points and "Y" seams.

- Match seams by placing turned appliqués on pieced blocks for perfect points.

- Paper-piece and machine or hand appliqué each block in less than an hour.

Create Paper-Pieced Appliqué Blocks in 5 Easy Steps

- Paper-piece the foundation block and remove foundation paper.

- Iron freezer paper to the wrong side of printed templates.

- Cut out and glue the paper template to the wrong side of the fabric. Turn with a glue stick.

- Stitch the appliqués, by hand or machine, to the foundation block to create the desired block.

- Remove the paper templates by soaking the block in warm water to dissolve the glue. Let the block dry and then press.

The Paper-Pieced Appliqué Process

Please read all the instructions even if you have paper-pieced in the past. Unique techniques have been developed to make it easy to create each of the blocks in less than an hour.

Preparing to Paper-Piece

Organize all the block pieces on a paper-plate before beginning. When the foundation paper, fabric, fussy-cut segments, and appliqués are prepared in advance, each block can be paper-pieced – start to finish – in less than an hour.

Read through each block's instructions before beginning and prepare the pieces in the following order:

- Copy and prepare the paper-piecing foundation paper

- Copy and prepare the paper templates, then prepare and turn the appliqués

- Copy and prepare the fussy cutting templates, if applicable, then cut the fussy-cut segments

- Cut out the fabric

When all the block pieces are prepared, place them on a paper plate in the order they will be sewn to the foundation paper. You have "kitted" the block and are ready to sew.

TIP

The fabric cutting instructions for the paper-pieced segments are included with each block. Many experienced paper-piecers use scraps, but cutting the fabric to the approximate size makes it easier. And, the finished blocks will be more stable since the grain line of the fabric has been taken into consideration.

Organize your sewing area so an iron, ironing board, rotary cutter, and mat are easily accessible. Each seam is pressed and trimmed before the next seam is sewn. You will also be trimming small amounts of fabric after each segment is pressed so have a waste basket handy.

Preparing the Block Foundation

When paper-piecing, the outline of the finished block is drawn on foundation paper. There are several brands of foundation paper available through your local quilt shop. I prefer a product similar to velum called Simple Foundations. With this type of paper, the numbers are visible on both sides. Regular copy paper can also be used, but you may find it more difficult to match the fussy-cut fabric segments.

Each block foundation in this book is labeled with the block name. The numbers indicate the order in which the fabric segments should be sewn to the foundation.

The letters represent the fabric in the block. For example, LB is light blue. Each block foundation and set of block instructions is labeled in this manner. If you are not using the fabric colors listed, replace the letters on the block foundation with ones to match the fabrics you are using in your project.

When the block has a fussy-cut segment, horizontal, diagonal, and vertical dashed lines are marked on the block foundation to aid in placing the fabric. The center of the Rambler foundation is one example.

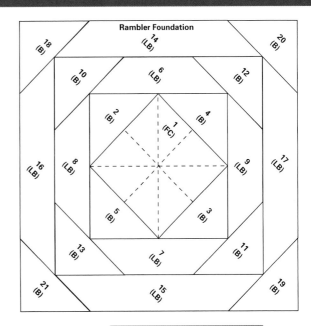

Rambler Foundation

TIPS

You will need one copy of the paper-piecing foundation for each block you wish to make

Some copiers distort images more than others. Check your copies for accuracy by comparing your foundations and templates to the ones in the book.

Make sure that the ink from your copies will not bleed and discolor the fabric when wet.

Supplies

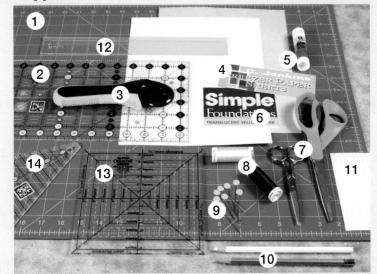

A minimal amount of supplies are needed to create the blocks and projects in this book. A few of the tools shown are optional, but they will make putting the blocks together easier.

Tools

1. Cutting mat
2. Acrylic ruler
3. Rotary cutter
4. Freezer paper
5. Water-soluble glue stick
6. Vellum paper
7. Scissors (small and large)
8. Monofilament thread
9. Pins
10. Marking pencils
11. Index card or other thin straight edge

Optional Tools

12. Add-A-Quarter™
13. Creative Grids® Square It Up & Fussy Cut ruler
14. Creative Grids® 45° Kaleidoscope & Dresden Plate ruler

Basic Paper-Piecing

Before beginning any of the blocks, make a copy of the paper-piecing foundation. Cut out the foundation on the outside lines of the block. Cut the fabrics, fussy cutting when indicated, according to the individual block instructions. In the example, the Rambler block is being shown.

Cutting and Preparing the Center Square

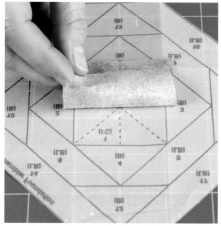

1 Cut a square of fabric approximately 1" larger than the foundation's center square. Center and glue the fabric right side up on the wrong side of the foundation.

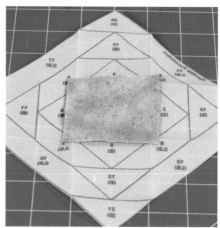

2 The fabric should extend approximately 1/2" over the square in all directions.

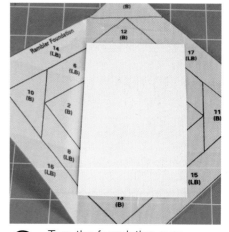

3 Turn the foundation over. Place the straight edge of something sturdy, such as template plastic, an index card, or manila folder, on one of the lines on the foundation center square.

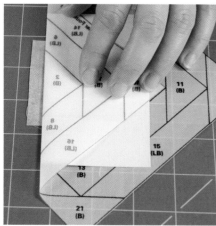

4 Fold the foundation back over the straight edge.

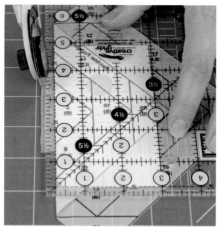

5 Trim the fabric 1/4" away from this fold using a ruler and rotary cutter.

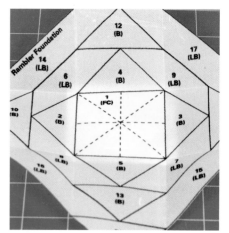

6 Continue in this manner to trim the remaining three sides of the center square. The fabric square is now 1/4" wider than the center square on all sides giving you an accurate seam allowance.

To fussy cut the Rambler block's center square, follow the instructions in Paper-Piecing with Fussy-Cut Segments on page 18. Whether or not you fussy cut the center square, the subsequent steps are the same. The example below shows a fussy-cut center square.

Rambler Block

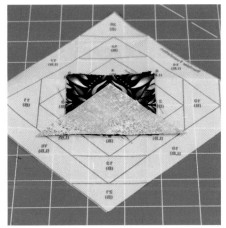

1 After the center square is in place, the remaining fabric segments are added in numerical order. Center and place the #2 triangle on the #1 center square, right sides together.

Note: Follow the cutting instructions for each individual block. Cutting the fabric pieces ensures that the cut segment is large enough to cover the paper-pieced segment and the outside edges will be on the straight of grain.

2 Place a dab of glue in the seam allowance to hold it in place.

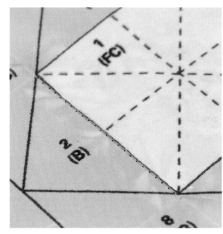

3 Turn the foundation over and sew on the line between the #1 and #2 pieces.

Note: You are only sewing on the line indicated. Do not stitch beyond that line.

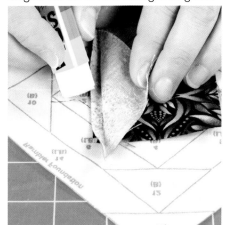

4 Turn the foundation over and press the #2 triangle over the foundation. Place a dab of glue within the #2 segment on the foundation to hold the fabric in place. Repeat the steps to add triangle #3.

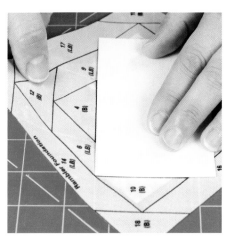

5 Turn the foundation over and place a straight edge on the line between the center square and the next fabric to be added—in this case #4.

Note: Whenever possible, the fabric segments are added to opposite sides so both can be sewn and pressed at one time.

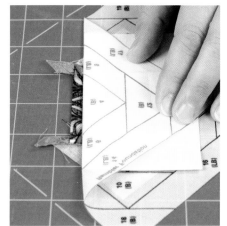

6 Fold the paper-piecing foundation back over the straight edge.

Basic Paper-Piecing, continued

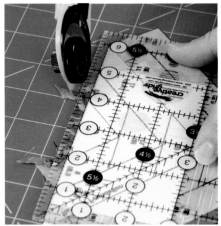

7 Trim the fabric 1/4" away from the folded edge using a ruler and rotary cutter.

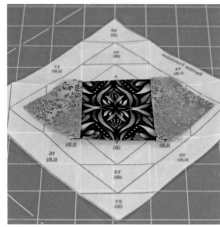

8 Repeat to trim the fabric on the other side.

9 Place the #4 and #5 triangles as shown. Place a dab of glue in the seam allowances to hold the triangles in place. Turn the foundation over and sew on the line between the #1 and #4 pieces and the #1 and #5 pieces.
Note: Both sides can be positioned and stitched at the same time if the triangle point is at least 1/4" away from the opposite side.

10 Press the triangles. Place a dab of glue within the #4 and #5 segments on the foundation to hold the fabric in place.

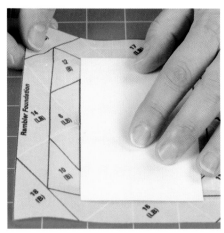

11 Turn the foundation over and place a straight edge on the line that separates #6 from the paper-pieced foundation block. Fold the foundation back over the straight edge.

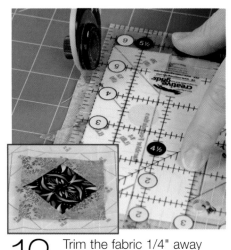

12 Trim the fabric 1/4" away from the folded edge using a ruler and rotary cutter.
Continue to trim all four sides to create a square in a square.

13 Place the #6 and #7 rectangle segments on the paper-pieced foundation block, right sides together. Add a dab of glue to hold them in place. Turn the foundation over and sew on the #6 and #7 lines. Press.

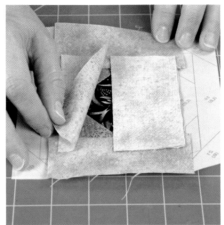

14 Place the #8 and #9 rectangle segments on the paper-pieced foundation block, right sides together. Turn the foundation over and sew on the #8 and #9 lines. Press.

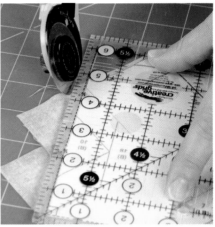

15 Turn the foundation over and place a straight edge on the #10 line. Fold back the foundation and trim the fabric 1/4" away from the fold using a ruler and rotary cutter.

16 Trim the remaining three sides. You once again have a square in a square.

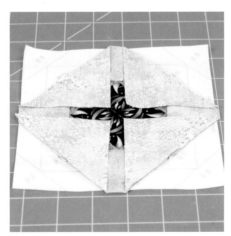

17 Now that the completed block is larger, the #10 - #13 triangles can all be positioned at the same time. Place a dab of glue on the pieces to hold in place. Turn the foundation over and sew on the #10, #11, #12 and #13 lines.

18 Press the triangles. Place a dab of glue within the #10 - #13 segments on the foundation to hold the fabric in place.

General Instructions

19 Turn the foundation over and place a straight edge on the #14 line. Fold back the foundation and trim 1/4" away from the fold using a ruler and rotary cutter. Repeat on the #15, #16 and #17 lines. Press.

20 Sew rectangles #14 - #17 to the foundation referring to steps 13-14. Place a straight edge on the #18 line, fold back the foundation and trim 1/4" away from the fold using a ruler and rotary cutter.

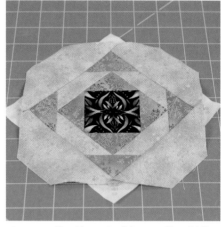

21 Continue to trim on the #19, #20 and #21 lines. Press.

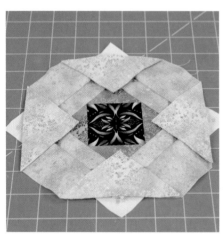

22 Sew triangles #18 - #21 to the foundation referring to steps 17-18.

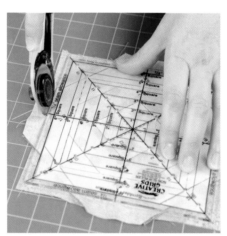

23 Place a 6-1/2" ruler on the foundation and trim all outside edges.

24 The finished paper-pieced Rambler block is perfect.

Preparing the Appliqué Templates

The appliqué templates are labeled with the name of the block and a letter which denotes placement order. The A templates are placed before the B templates, and so on. The starred (*) edges of the templates indicate that these edges need to be turned.

The numbered templates are used when paper-piecing with fussy-cut segments. Refer to page 18.

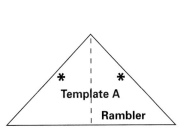

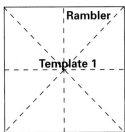

To make the paper templates for the appliqués, photocopy the template patterns for each block or trace the template patterns onto white copy paper.

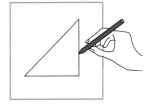

Note: To download a complete set of templates for the blocks in this book, visit landauerpub.com/Quilt-Block-Fusion-Penny-Haren.html.

Adding the Freezer Paper

Place the photocopied paper templates face down on the ironing board. Place the waxy side of the freezer paper on top of the **BLANK** side of the copied paper templates. Press with a dry iron. This double layer of paper creates a very crisp template that is easy to remove in one piece. It is also easier to turn the fabric over the template without distorting the original shape. I prefer C. Jenkins™ 8-1/2" x 11" Freezer Paper Sheets available through your local quilt shop.

Cutting Out the Paper Templates

When cutting out the paper templates, cut just **INSIDE** the photocopied or drawn lines to allow for the thickness of the fabric when it is turned over the template.

Preparing the Fabric Appliqué

Glue the **BLANK** side of the freezer paper template onto the wrong side of the fabric. The printing on the freezer paper template should be face up.

Using a rotary cutter and ruler, trim the fabric exactly 1/4" away from the template on all sides. By trimming 1/4" away, you are adding an accurate seam allowance to the appliqué which will help you position the appliqué on the paper-pieced block.

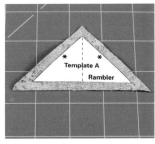

All curved sides on a template are turned. Estimate the 1/4" seam allowance on those edges.

Note: Since the paper foundations and templates do not include the seam allowance, they can be enlarged or reduced to any size you wish. Adjust the cutting instructions accordingly.

TIP

Some printers will shrink the templates to fit preset margins. Run one copy and check it against the templates in the book to be sure they are printing at 100%.

If your copier distorts the pattern too much, you will have to trace the pattern onto white typing paper or find another copier. My own copier tends to distort in one direction about 1/16". I can live with that.

General Instructions

Paper-Piecing with Fussy-Cut Segments

Many paper-pieced blocks begin with a center square. Choosing a specific design in the fabric, and cutting it so it is featured in the finished block, is called fussy cutting. Fussy cutting can add drama and interest to a block. Templates for fussy cutting segments are included in many of the blocks if you wish to incorporate this technique into your projects.

When a segment is fussy cut, a template the exact size of the finished paper-pieced segment is provided. This template includes dashed horizontal, vertical, and diagonal lines to aid in placing it on the fabric. I prefer to copy these templates on Simple Foundations paper. Since this paper is translucent, it can be placed directly over the foundation paper allowing you to match the dashed lines. See step 4 on page 19.

TIP

Before choosing the design to fussy cut, consider the final layout of the quilt. If the block is going to be set on point in the finished project, the design should be cut so it is set on point as well.

Preparing the Fussy-Cut Segments

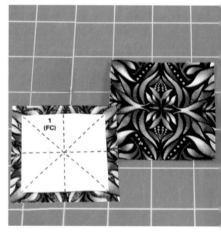

1 Place a dab of glue on the fussy cut template and place it on the chosen design in the fabric.

2 Trim the fabric exactly 1/4" away from the template on all sides.

3 After the template is trimmed, the design should be centered on the square as shown.

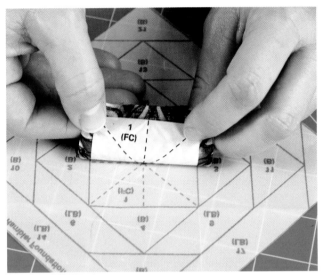

4 Since the fussy-cut segment is cut out of foundation paper, it does not need to be removed. Place the template directly over the center square on the block foundation, matching the dashed lines.

5 The fabric will be centered in your finished block. Continue paper-piecing the block, referring to pages 13-16.

Turning the Appliqués

Turning Straight Edges and Corners

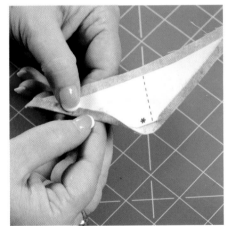

1 Run a glue stick along the edge of the paper template and the edge of the fabric to be turned. Be sure to run the glue past the template into the seam allowance.

2 Turn the edge of the wrong side of the fabric over the template using your thumbnail and moving forward 1/8" at a time.

3 At the corner turn seam allowance down slightly to conceal and neaten the beginning of the turned second side. Continue to turn the second side 1/8" at a time using your thumbnail.

Note: In block instructions the sides of the templates to be turned are marked with an ∗. Unturned sides are the seam allowances.

Turning the Appliqués, continued

Turning Triangles

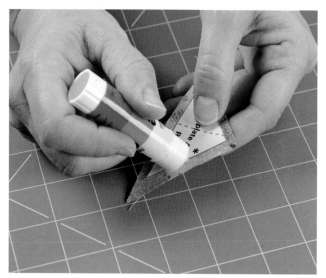

1 Run a glue stick along the edge of the paper template and the edge of the fabric to be turned. Be sure to run the glue past the template into the seam allowance.

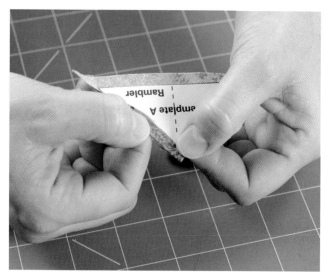

2 Turn the edge of the wrong side of the fabric over the template using your thumbnail and moving forward 1/8" at a time. At the corner turn the fabric so it is angled slightly down. This will create "tails" on the bottom raw edge of the triangle.

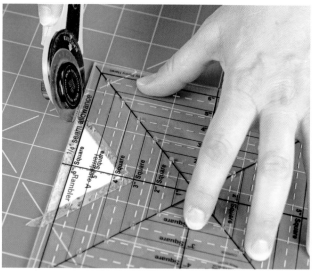

3 Trim the tails even with the seam allowance.

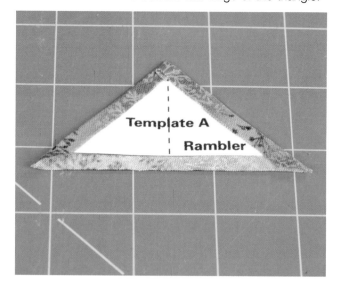

TIP

I use white paste glue sticks to turn my appliqués. Don't purchase the purple, pink, and blue ones. You don't want to risk dyes coming back at a later date. Buy the large packages of glue sticks and keep them in the refrigerator. The moist environment stops them from drying out and they will last up to a year. When you are not using your glue stick, put the lid back on. They dry out very quickly if you leave the top off while turning each piece.

Turning Outside Curves

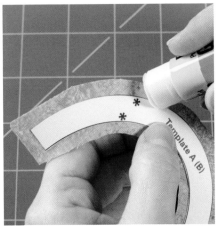 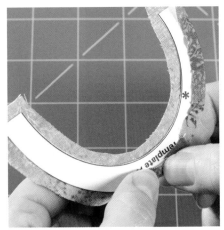 

Some blocks have appliqués with curves. When turning an outside curve, trim the fabric approximately 1/4" away from the curved side of the template. Glue along the outside edge of the curve. Turn and gather the fabric around the template. Do not clip outside curves. If you have rough edges on your appliqué, turn it over to the wrong side. You will notice there are pleats on the folded edge of your piece. While the glue is still wet, place a fingernail on each side of the "pleat" and pull it down to the correct shape.

• •

Turning Inside Curves

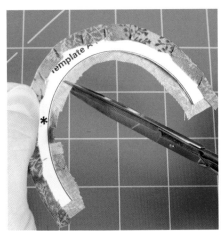 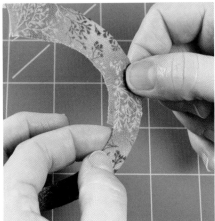 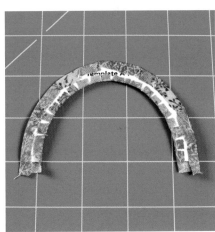

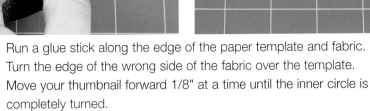

1   In the picture above, the center circle must be cut out approximately 1/4" away from the inner circle of the template. The seam allowance must be clipped in order to turn the fabric over the template.

2   Run a glue stick along the edge of the paper template and fabric. Turn the edge of the wrong side of the fabric over the template. Move your thumbnail forward 1/8" at a time until the inner circle is completely turned.

Stitching the Appliqué Templates

Thread

Use only high quality cotton or cotton-wrapped polyester thread. Not all threads are created equal.

Hand Stitching

Hand stitch the turned edges of the appliqué, using an invisible appliqué stitch. Leave the raw edges open. Take a few extra stitches to reinforce any areas that were clipped because of inside curves. Do not place your knot on the wrong side of the foundation square. The thread tail could shadow through the finished block. Knots should be hidden beneath the appliqué piece.

Machine Stitching

 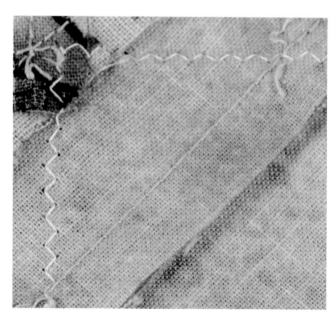

If you prefer to machine stitch, use a narrow zigzag stitch with invisible thread in the top of your machine and 50 or 60 weight thread in the bobbin. Remove the paper templates and glue, following the directions on page 23.

Removing the Paper Templates and Glue

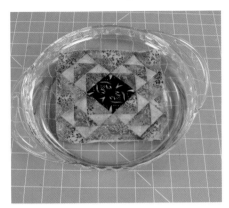

1 When the stitching is done, place the appliquéd block into warm water for at least twenty minutes. This will dissolve the glue.

2 Remove the appliquéd block from the water and squeeze out the excess water.

3 Roll the block in an absorbent towel to remove any remaining water.

4 Smooth the block out on the towel and let dry before removing the paper templates. Pull out the paper templates along the raw edges of the block.

5 If necessary, run the seams under water to flush out any remaining glue. Smooth the block out again and press.

TIPS

Place several completed blocks in a sink of warm water at night and remove paper templates in the morning. If you are afraid the fabrics may bleed, add a color grabber sheet.

Press your completed appliqué blocks on a folded bath towel. Spray each piece with spray starch and press the wrong side to guarantee that all seams are pressed correctly. Then press the right side. The spray starch gives it a crisp look, reduces distortion and fraying, and protects the finished block.

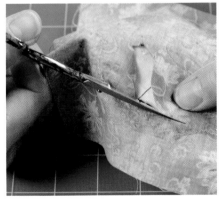

1 To remove inside templates, slit or cut the background fabric. Avoid cutting through the appliquéd stitches.

2 Remove the inside paper templates. Cut away any excess fabric if you are going to hand quilt or if the foundation block will shadow through the completed block.

3 Smooth the block out again and press.

Basket Block

The basket block is created by combining two paper-piecing techniques. The basket base is paper-pieced with pieced segments and the handle is adding using the flipped back appliqué technique. Begin by cutting the fabrics for the block referring to the Basket block instructions on page 48. Next, prepare the pieced segments and appliqué so you have everything you need to start the paper-piecing process.

1 Sew the #2A triangle base to the #2B background rectangle to form a pieced segment. Press the seams open. Repeat with #3A and #3B.

Note: When a segment is pieced, it is numbered as a set. For example, the segments become #2A/#2B and #3A/#3B.

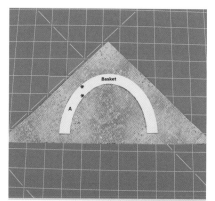

2 Glue Template A to the wrong side of a triangle. Since the template is placed on a triangle, minimal clipping is required because the curve is on the bias.

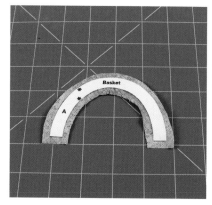

3 Trim the fabric 1/4" away from the paper template on all sides. The curves can be approximate but the straight base needs to be exactly 1/4" since it will be placed in the seam allowance. Clip the inside curve. Run glue along the curves of the template and turn. Do not turn the straight base. Set aside.

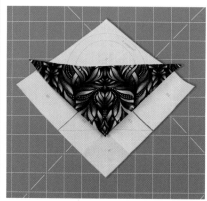

4 Place a dab of glue on the wrong side of the #1 section of the paper-piecing foundation block. Center the base triangle on the #1 section, right side up. Trim the triangle 1/4" away from the drawn lines on the foundation following Basic Paper-Piecing steps 3-6 on page 12.

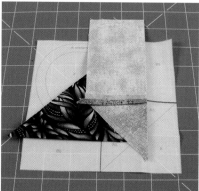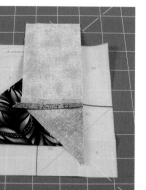

5 You may wish to trace the seam line between #2A/#2B on the wrong side of the paper-piecing foundation to assist with placement of the segment. Place the seam line of the #2A/#2B pieced segment on the triangle, right sides together, and lining up with the traced line. Place a dab of glue in the seam allowance to hold the pieces in place. Turn the foundation over and sew on the line separating the #1 and #2A/#2B segments. Press. Repeat to add the #3A/#3B segment.

Press the pieced segments away from the base triangle and trim.

Basket Block

6 Paper-piece #4. Press and trim.

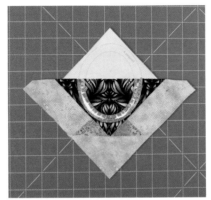

7 Place the A appliqué on the basket base, right sides together. The appliqué should fit within the triangle and not overlap any of the other fabrics.

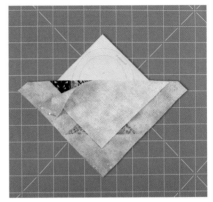

8 With right sides together, place the #5 fabric triangle on the basket base triangle, sandwiching the A appliqué between them.

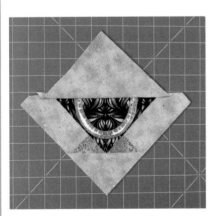

9 Paper-piece #5 and press.

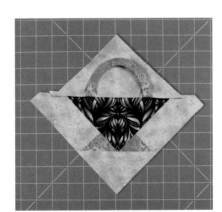

10 Flip the A appliqué back over the #5 triangle and glue in place.

11 Trim the fabric 1/4" away from the paper-pieced foundation. Remove the foundation paper. Appliqué the handle in place referring to page 22. Follow the instructions on page 23 to remove the template and glue. Press. Trim the finished block to 6-1/2".

Watch Penny demonstrate this technique at landauerpub.com/Quilt-Block-Fusion-Penny-Haren.html.

Central Park Block

The Central Park block is created with a simple paper-pieced foundation and strip-pieced appliqués. Central Park's strip-pieced appliqués are made from a two fabric strip set.

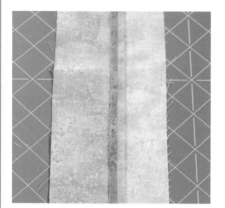

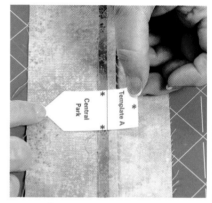

1 Sew two fabric strips together as shown. Press the seam open.

Note: *Refer to individual blocks for cutting instructions. This example uses the Central Park block on page 36.*

2 Apply glue to the wrong side of the paper template.

3 Place the template on the pieced fabric strip. The line on the template should be placed on the seam line of the strip.

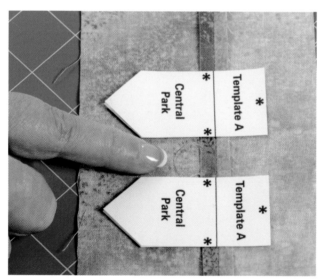

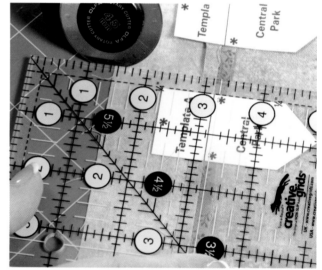

4 Position the templates at least a finger's width apart to allow for the seam allowance to be cut around each template.

Note: *Your finger is approximately 1/2" wide and is a good measurement for spacing the templates.*

5 Separate the templates by trimming the fabric 1/4" away from the long sides of the templates.

Watch Penny demonstrate this technique at landauerpub.com/Quilt-Block-Fusion-Penny-Haren.html.

STRIP-PIECED APPLIQUÉS

Central Park Block

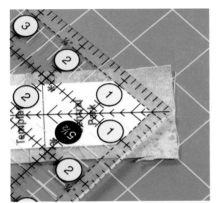

6 Trim the remaining fabric on the templates 1/4" on all sides.

Note: *If you are using the Creative Grids® 6-1/2" Turn-a-Round ruler, you can trim both sides of the point at the same time.*

7 Run glue along the edges of the template marked with an "★" and turn. Do not turn the points.

8 Glue the strip-pieced appliqués in place on the paper-pieced foundation, lining up the points of the appliqué with the corner of the paper-pieced foundation.

9 The center square is now an octagon and you didn't have to sew any inset seams.

Appliqué in place referring to page 22. Follow the instructions on page 23 to remove the templates and glue. Press.

The pointed Dresden Plate is created by cutting eight 45° triangles – four each of two coordinating fabrics. Since a circle is appliquéd over the center of the pieced segments, they are cut and pieced so a hole is created in the center. This "hole" eliminates the bulk in the center of the Dresden Plate.

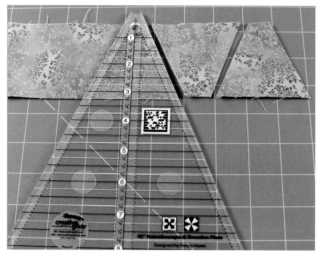

Cutting 45° Segments

Cut a 2-3/4" strip of coordinating fabric from selvage to selvage. Line up the 3-1/4" line on the Creative Grids® 45° Kaleidoscope and Dresden Plate ruler with the bottom of the strip. The ruler will extend 1/2" beyond the top of the fabric. This will create the hole when the segments are pieced together. Cut along the edges of the ruler to cut a segment. Rotate the ruler 180° and continue cutting segments. Four of these segments are needed for each block. You can layer the strips and cut multiple segments at one time.

Fussy Cutting Segments

Fussy cut a 2-3/4" strip of coordinating fabric. Place the ruler's center line on a design element in the strip. Cut four segments by placing the 3-1/4" line on the ruler on the bottom of the strip. Depending on your focal fabric, you may be able to rotate the ruler 180° and fussy cut the segments for a different block.

Note: Templates for this block are provided on page 52 if you choose not to use the ruler shown.

1 Fold each segment in half vertically and finger press. Sew a 1/4" seam across the top of each segment.

2 Place your thumb on the seam and turn the point right side out. By holding the seam, the stitches will not come loose when putting stress on the seam while turning. Do not clip the point before turning. Turn the seam to one side and use a blunt tip to create the point.

POINTED DRESDEN PLATE

3 Line up the seam with the finger pressed vertical crease and press.

4 Matching the points, place a fussy-cut and plain segment right sides together. The bottom flat tips will be covered by the center appliqué so they do not need to match. Always layer the same fabric segment on top so the fabrics will alternate when the Dresden Plate block is pieced. Sew and press the seams open.

5 Matching the outer points, layer two pairs of segments right sides together, alternating the fabrics. Sew these segments together along one edge to create two halves of the Dresden Plate.

6 Sew these two halves together to complete the Dresden Plate.

7 Turn the circle template and place on the center of the Dresden Plate to cover the hole. Appliqué in place on the background fabric referring to page 22. Follow the instructions on page 23 to remove the template and glue. Press.

Watch Penny demonstrate this technique at landauerpub.com/Quilt-Block-Fusion-Penny-Haren.html.

ROUND DRESDEN PLATE

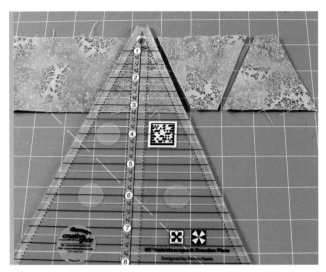

Cutting 45° Segments

Cut a 2-3/4" strip of coordinating fabric from selvage to selvage. Line up the 3-1/4" line on the Creative Grids® 45° Kaleidoscope and Dresden Plate ruler with the bottom of the strip. The ruler will extend 1/2" beyond the top of the fabric. This will create the hole when the segments are pieced together. Cut along the edges of the ruler to cut a segment. Rotate the ruler 180° and continue cutting segments. Four of these segments are needed for each block. You can layer the strips and cut multiple segments at one time.

Fussy Cutting Segments

Fussy cut a 2-3/4" strip. Place the ruler's center line on a design element in the strip. Cut four segments by placing the 3-1/4" line on the ruler on the bottom of the strip. Depending on your focal fabric, you may be able to rotate the ruler 180° and fussy cut the segments for a different block.

Note: *Templates for this block are provided on page 52 if you choose not to use the ruler shown.*

1 Matching the wide tops, place a plain and fussy-cut segment right sides together. The bottom flat tips will be covered by the center appliqué so don't worry if they don't match. Always place the same fabric segment on top so the fabrics will alternate when the Dresden Plate block is pieced. Sew and press the seams open.

2 Matching the wide tops, place pairs of segments right sides together. Sew together along one edge to create two halves of the Dresden Plate. Press the seams open.

3 Sew these two halves together to complete the Dresden Plate. Press the seams open.

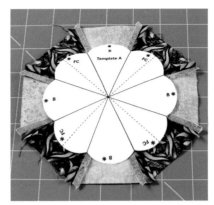

4 Place the template on the wrong side of the pieced Dresden Plate matching the lines on the template to the seam lines. Glue in place.

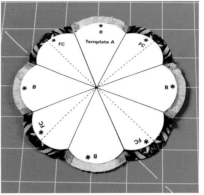

5 Trim the fabric 1/4" away from the template on all sides.

6 Pull a few threads out at each seam. Run a glue stick around the outside edge and turn.

7 Turn the circle template and place on the center of the Dresden Plate to cover the hole. Appliqué in place on the background fabric referring to page 22. Follow the instructions on page 23 to remove the templates and glue. Press.

Watch Penny demonstrate this technique at landauerpub.com/Quilt-Block-Fusion-Penny-Haren.html.

Make traditional looking Grandmother's Flower Garden blocks in less than half the time with this strip-pieced technique. The strip in the center allows you to fussy cut the center of the flower.

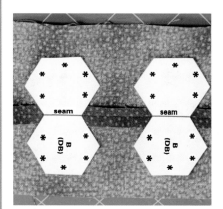

1 Sew two matching fabric strips together along the long edges as shown. Press the seam open. Glue the B paper templates to the wrong side of the strip-pieced unit matching the line on the templates to the seam line on the strip-pieced unit. Place templates at least 1/2" apart.

Note: *Refer to page 32 for block cutting instructions.*

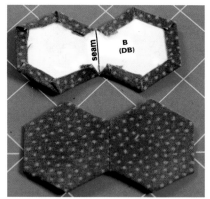

2 Trim the fabric 1/4" away from the paper templates on all sides. Turn all sides of the appliqués.

Note: *Sewing two of the same fabric strips together replicates the seam that would show if doing this block traditionally.*

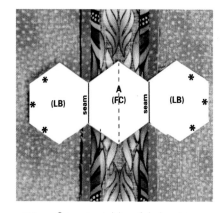

3 Sew matching fabric strips to opposite sides of a fussy-cut strip along the long edges. Press the seams open. Glue paper template A to the wrong side of the strip-pieced unit. Match the lines on the templates to the seam lines on the strip-pieced unit and center the template over a design in the fussy-cut strip.

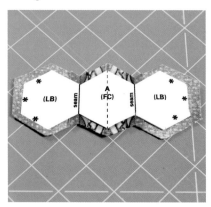

4 Trim the fabric 1/4" away from the paper template on all sides.

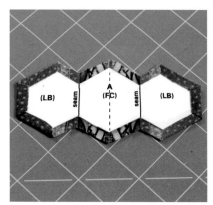

5 Turn the three outside edges on each end of the appliqué.

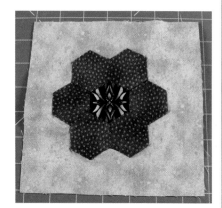

6 Place a B appliqué on opposite sides of the A appliqué. Match the seam lines and glue in place. Appliqué the overlapping seams and the flower edges in place on the background fabric referring to page 22. Follow the instructions on page 23 to remove the templates and glue. Press.

Watch Penny demonstrate this technique at landauerpub.com/Quilt-Block-Fusion-Penny-Haren.html.

Traditionally, the Grandmother's Flower Garden block is pieced together by hand. With this easy technique the block is pieced on the machine, saving time and allowing the hexagons to be fussy cut.

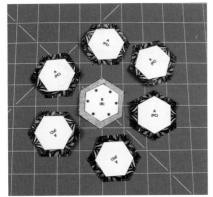

1 Cut out six A paper templates and one B paper template on page 53. Glue the six A templates to the wrong side of the fussy-cut fabric, placing each over the same design. Glue B template to the wrong side of a solid fabric. Trim the fabric 1/4" away from the paper templates on all sides.

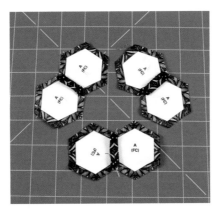

2 Matching the fabric design, place two A appliqués, right sides together, and glue in place. Do not put glue in the seam allowance. Sew along the edge of the paper templates and press the seam open. Make three sets of A appliqués.

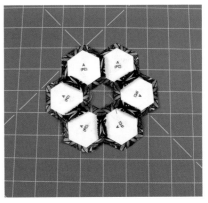

3 Sew the three sets of A appliqués together to form the flower. Press the seams open.

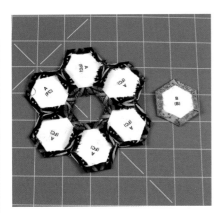

4 Turn the outside edges of the flower. Turn all the edges of the B appliqué.

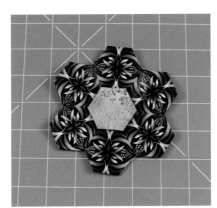

5 Using a dab of glue, center the B appliqué in place on the flower.

6 Appliqué the pieces in place on the background fabric referring to page 22. Follow the instructions on page 23 to remove the templates and glue. Press.

Rambler

Techniques

Techniques featured in this block include:

- Basic Paper-Piecing
- Pieced Appliqué
- Paper-Piecing with Fussy-Cut Segments

For information on these techniques, turn to pages 12, 17 and 18.

Fabrics

Focus Fabric (FC):
Paper-Piece #1
Fussy cut 1—3" square

Light Blue (LB):
Paper-Piece #6, #7, #8, #9, #14, #15, #16, #17
Cut 1—2" strip, selvage to selvage
Sub cut the strip into:
    4—2" x 4" segments (#6, #7, #8, #9) and
    4—2" x 6" segments (#14, #15, #16, #17)

Bronze (B):
Paper-Piece #2, #3, #4, #5, #10, #11, #12, #13, #18, #19, #20, #21
Cut 6—3" squares
Cut each square once on the diagonal

Appliqué A
Cut 2—4" squares
Cut each square once on the diagonal

Refer to General Instructions on pages 10-23 before beginning this block.

Watch Penny demonstrate the techniques used to make this block at landauerpub.com/Quilt-Block-Fusion-Penny-Haren.html.

CUTTING THE PAPER TEMPLATES

Cut 4 Template A on page 50.

Note: *The cutting instructions are optional. You may choose to paper-piece this block with scraps. However, if you are new to paper-piecing, cutting the fabric to the approximate size will make it easier. The finished block will also be more stable because the grain line of the fabric has been taken into consideration.*
A fussy-cut template (Template 1) is included if you would like to fussy cut the center design. Refer to page 18 for detailed instructions on fussy cutting.

Make one copy of the paper-piecing foundation on page 50. Do **not** include a seam allowance when cutting out the paper-piecing foundation.

PIECING

This block consists of 25 pieces.

1 Glue the A paper templates to the wrong side of a scrap of bronze fabric. Trim the fabric 1/4" away from the templates on all sides. Turn the "✦" sides of each appliqué.

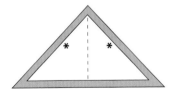

Template A

2 Paper-piece #1 through #21 following Basic Paper-Piecing instructions on pages 12-16.

3 Trim the fabric 1/4" away from the paper-piecing foundation. Remove the foundation paper from the paper-pieced block.

4 Glue the A appliqués on the paper-pieced block.

5 Appliqué in place, leaving raw edges open. Follow the directions on page 23 to remove the paper templates and glue. Press.

Central Park

Techniques

Techniques featured in this block include:

- Basic Paper-Piecing
- Paper-Piecing with Fussy-Cut Segments
- Strip-Pieced Appliqués

For information on these techniques, turn to pages 12, 18 and 26.

Fabrics

Focus Fabric (FC):
Paper-Piece #1
Fussy cut 1—4" square

Bronze (B):
Appliqué A
Cut 1—2-1/2" x 9" strip

Dot (D):
Paper-Piece #6, #7, #8, #9
Cut 1—2" x 30" strip
Sub cut the strip into:
    2—2" x 6" rectangles (#6; #7) and
    2—2" x 7" rectangles (#8; #9)

Light Blue (LB):
Paper-Piece #2, #3, #4, #5
Cut 1—1-1/2" x 22" strip
Sub cut the strip into:
    2—1-1/2" x 4" rectangles (#2, #3) and
    2—1-1/2" x 5-1/2" rectangles (#4, #5)

Appliqué A
Cut 1—2" x 9" strip

Refer to General Instructions on pages 10-23 before beginning this block.

Watch Penny demonstrate the techniques used to make this block at landauerpub.com/Quilt-Block-Fusion-Penny-Haren.html.

CUTTING THE PAPER TEMPLATES

Cut 4 Template A on page 51. The A appliqués are pieced from the bronze and light blue fabric.

Note: The cutting instructions are optional. You may choose to paper-piece this block with scraps. However, if you are new to paper-piecing, cutting the fabric to the approximate size will make it easier. The finished block will also be more stable because the grain line of the fabric has been taken into consideration. A fussy-cut template (Template 1) is included if you would like to fussy cut the center design. Refer to page 18 for detailed instructions on fussy cutting.

Make one copy of the paper-piecing foundation on page 51. Do **not** include a seam allowance when cutting out the paper-piecing foundations.

PIECING

This block consists of 17 pieces.

1 Sew the 2" light blue strip to the 2-1/2" bronze strip along the length of the strip. Press the seam open. Glue the A paper templates to the wrong side of the pieced strip set, matching the line on the templates to the seam line on the pieced strip set. Trim the fabric 1/4" away from the templates on all sides.

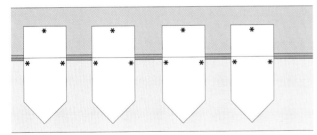

Template A

2 Turn the "⋆" sides of each appliqué.

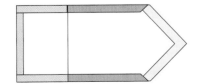

3 Paper-piece #1 through #9 following Basic Paper-Piecing instructions on pages 12-16. Trim the fabric 1/4" away from the paper-pieced foundation. Remove the foundation paper from the paper-pieced block.

4 Glue the pieced A appliqués on the paper-pieced block.

5 Appliqué in place, leaving raw edges open. Follow the directions on page 23 to remove the paper templates and glue. Press.

Pointed Dresden Plate

Techniques

Techniques featured in this block include:

- Pieced Appliqué
- Fussy-Cut Segments
- Pointed Dresden Plate

For information on these techniques, turn to pages 17, 18 and 28.

Fabrics

Focus Fabric (FC):
Cut 1—2-3/4" x 21" strip
Note: Depending on the repeat of the motif you are fussy cutting, the strip may need to be longer.

Bronze (B):
Cut 1—2-3/4" x 18" strip

Medium Blue (MB):
Cut 1—7" Square for the block background

Dark Blue (DB):
Appliqué A
Scrap to cut 1

Refer to General Instructions on pages 10-23 before beginning this block.

Watch Penny demonstrate the techniques used to make this block at landauerpub.com/Quilt-Block-Fusion-Penny-Haren.html.

CUTTING THE PAPER TEMPLATES

Cut one Template A on page 52.

Note: *If you are not using a 45° ruler, a triangle template is provided on page 52.*

CUTTING THE 45° TRIANGLES

Note: *The block will consist of four bronze segments and four fussy-cut segments. Cut four matching fussy-cut fabric segments so they match within the block.*

1 Cut a 45° segment from the bronze fabric strip, lining up the 3-1/4" line on the ruler with the bottom edge of the fabric. The wider tip will result in a "hole" in the center of the plate when the segments are sewn together. This "hole" will be covered by a circle appliqué after the Dresden Plate is pieced. Continue to rotate the ruler 180°, lining up the angled edge of the ruler with the angled edge of the fabric to cut a total of four triangles.

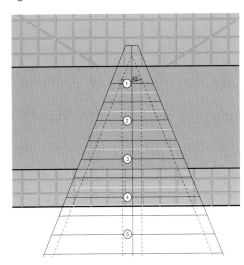

2 To fussy cut the 45° segments, place the ruler's center line on the center of a design in the fussy-cut strip. Line up the 3-1/4" line on the ruler with the bottom edge of the fabric. The wider tip will result in a "hole" in the center of the plate when the segments are sewn together. This "hole" will be covered by a circle appliqué after the Dresden Plate is pieced. Continue to rotate the ruler 180°, lining up the center line on the ruler with the center of a design to cut a total of 4 triangles. Refer to the Pointed Dresden Plate Technique Notebook on page 28 for information on fussy cutting the segments.

PIECING

This block consists of 10 pieces.

1 Glue the A paper template to the wrong side of a scrap of dark blue fabric. Trim the fabric 1/4" away from the template on all sides. Turn the entire circle.

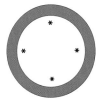

Template A

2 Fold each 45° segment in half vertically, right sides together, and finger-press. Sew a 1/4" seam across the top of each segment.

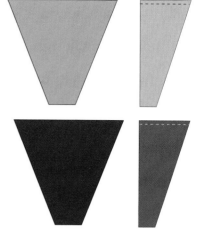

3 Turn each segment right side out. Center the seam on the finger-pressed center of the segment and press.

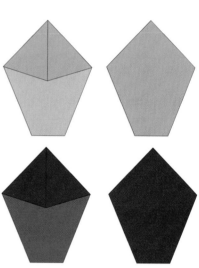

4 Place a bronze segment on a fussy-cut segment, right sides together. Be sure to match the segments at the pointed end. The flat ends will be covered by an appliqué so they do not need to be perfect. Sew along the angled side with a 1/4" seam allowance. The bronze segment must always be on top when sewing segments together. Make four sets. Press the seams open.

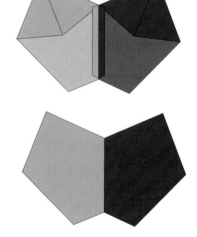

5 Sew the sets together in pairs, alternating fabrics. Press the seams open.

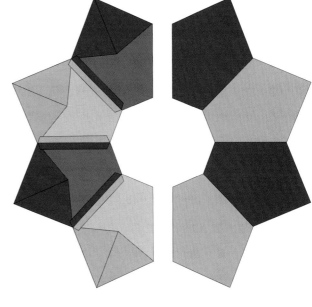

6 Sew the two pieces together to complete the Dresden Plate.

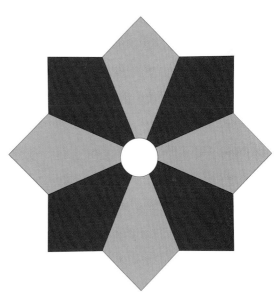

7 Center and glue the Dresden Plate on the medium blue fabric square. Glue the A appliqué over the Dresden Plate covering the center hole. Appliqué the pieces in place.

8 Follow the directions on page 23 to remove the paper templates and glue. Trim the finished block to 6-1/2" and press.

Round Dresden Plate

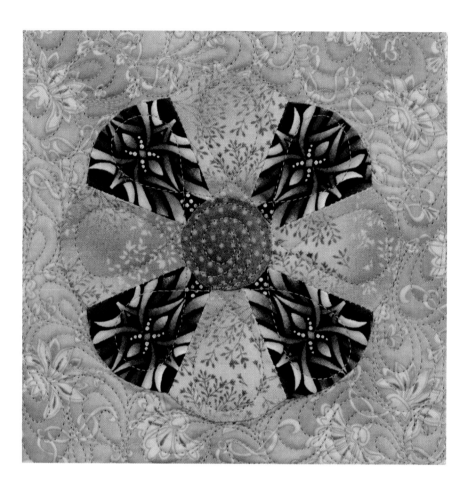

Techniques

Techniques featured in this block include:

• Pieced Appliqué
• Fussy-Cut Segments
• Round Dresden Plate

For information on these techniques, turn to pages 17, 18 and 30.

Fabrics

Focus Fabric (FC):
Cut 1—2-3/4" x 21" strip
Note: Depending on the repeat of the motif you are fussy cutting, the strip may need to be longer.

Bronze (B):
Cut 1—2-3/4" x 18" strip

Medium Blue (MB):
Cut 1—7" Square for the block background

Dark Blue (DB):
Appliqué A
Scrap to cut 1

Refer to General Instructions on pages 10-23 before beginning this block.

Watch Penny demonstrate the techniques used to make this block at landauerpub.com/Quilt-Block-Fusion-Penny-Haren.html.

CUTTING THE PAPER TEMPLATES

Cut one Template A and B on page 52.

Note: *If you are not using a 45° ruler, a triangle template is provided on page 52.*

CUTTING THE 45° TRIANGLES

Note: *The block will consist of four bronze segments and four fussy-cut segments. Cut four matching fussy-cut fabric segments so they match within the block.*

1 Cut a 45° segment from the bronze fabric strip, lining up the 3-1/4" line on the ruler with the bottom edge of the fabric. The wider tip will result in a "hole" in the center of the plate when the segments are sewn together. This "hole" will be covered by a circle appliqué after the Dresden Plate is pieced. Continue to rotate the ruler 180°, lining up the angled edge of the ruler with the angled edge of the fabric to cut a total of four triangles.

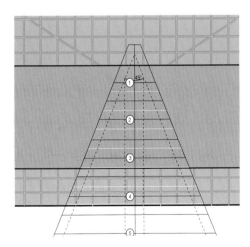

2 To fussy cut the 45° segments, place the ruler's center line on the center of a design in the fussy-cut strip. Line up the 3-1/4" line on the ruler with the bottom edge of the fabric. The wider tip will result in a "hole" in the center of the plate when the segments are sewn together. This "hole" will be covered by a circle appliqué after the Dresden Plate is pieced. Continue to rotate the ruler 180°, lining up the center line on the ruler with the center of a design to cut a total of 4 triangles. Refer to the Round Dresden Plate Technique Notebook on page 30 for information on fussy cutting the segments.

PIECING

This block consists of 10 pieces.

1 Glue the B paper template to the wrong side of the scrap of dark blue fabric. Trim the fabric 1/4" away from the templates on all sides. Turn the entire circle.

Template B

2 Sew a fussy-cut segment to a bronze segment with right sides together. Sew a total of four sets. Press the seams open.

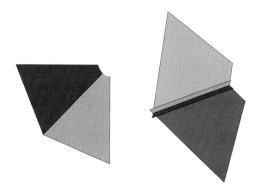

3 Sew two sets of segments together. Press the seams open.

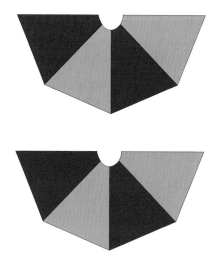

4 Sew the two pieces together. Press the seam open. The hole in the center will be covered by the B appliqué.

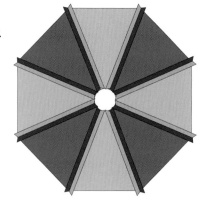
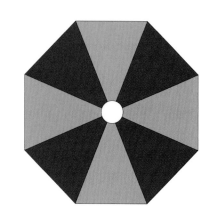

5 Glue the A paper template to the wrong side of the pieced ring, matching the lines on the template with the seam lines on the pieced ring.

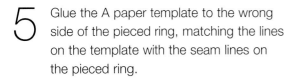

6 Trim the fabric 1/4" away from the template.

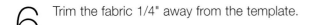

7 Turn the fabric over the outside edges of the template.

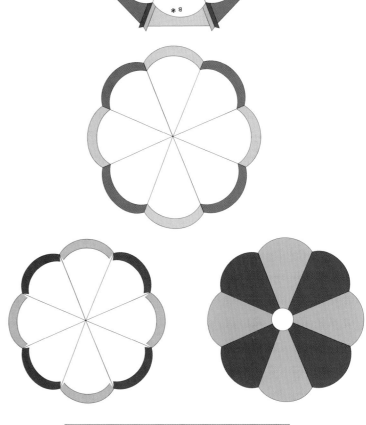

8 Center and glue the Dresden Plate on the medium blue fabric square. Glue the B appliqué over the Dresden Plate covering the center hole. Appliqué the pieces in place.

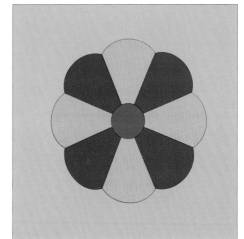

9 Follow the directions on page 23 to remove the paper templates and glue. Trim the finished block to 6-1/2" and press.

Grandmother's Flower Garden

Techniques

Techniques featured in this block include:

- Pieced Appliqué
- Fussy-Cut Segments
- Strip-Pieced Appliqué

For information on these techniques, turn to pages 17, 18 and 26.

Fabrics

Focus Fabric (FC):
Fussy cut 1—2" x 3" unit

Light Blue (LB):
Cut 1—7" square for the block background

Dark Blue (DB):
Cut 2—2-1/2" x 6" strips
2—2-1/2" x 3" units

Refer to General Instructions on pages 10-23 before beginning this block.

Watch Penny demonstrate the techniques used to make this block at landauerpub.com/Quilt-Block-Fusion-Penny-Haren.html.

CUTTING THE PAPER TEMPLATES

Cut 1 Template A and 2 Template B on page 53.

Note: *The A and B appliqués are cut from strip-pieced units.*

PIECING

This block consists of 3 pieces.

1 Sew a 2-1/2" x 3" dark blue fabric unit to opposite long edges of the 2" fussy cut unit. Press the seams open.

2 Glue the A paper template to the wrong side of the strip-pieced unit, matching the line on the template to the seam line on the strip-pieced unit. The center hexagon on the template should be centered on a motif in the fussy-cut strip.

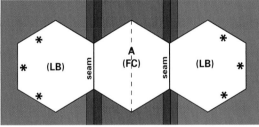

Template A

3 Trim the fabric 1/4" away from the template on all sides. Turn the "⋆" sides of each appliqué.

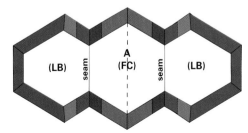

4 Sew 2—2-1/2" x 6" dark blue fabric strips together along the long edges. Press the seam open.

Note: *Sewing two of the same fabric strips together replicates the seam that would show if doing this block traditionally.*

5 Glue the B paper templates to the wrong side of the strip-pieced unit, matching the line on the templates to the seam line on the strip-pieced units.

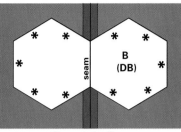

Template B

6 Trim the fabric 1/4" away from the templates on all sides. Turn the "⋆" sides of each appliqué.

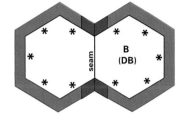 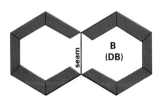

7 Place a B appliqué on opposite sides of an A appliqué. Match the seam lines and glue in place.

8 Stitch the appliqués together to create the Grandmother's Flower Garden block.

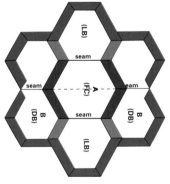 

9 Center the block on the background fabric square. Appliqué in place.

10 Follow the directions on page 23 to remove the paper templates and glue. Trim the finished block to 6-1/2" and press.

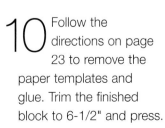 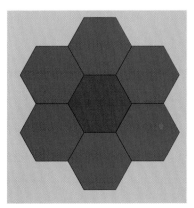

Basket

Techniques

Techniques featured in this block include:

• Basic Paper-Piecing
• Pieced Appliqué
• Paper-Piecing with a
  Flipped Back Appliqué
• Paper-Piecing with
  Pieced Segments

For information on these techniques, turn to pages 12, 17 and 24.

Fabrics

Focus Fabric (FC):
Paper-Piece #1
Fussy cut 1—6" square
Cut square in half once
on the diagonal

Bronze (B):
Paper-Piece #2A, #3A
Cut 1—4" square
Cut square in quarters twice
on the diagonal
Appliqué A
Cut 1—6" square
Cut square in half once
on the diagonal

Light Blue (LB):
Paper-Piece #2B, #3B
Cut 2—2-1/2" x 4-1/2" rectangles
Paper-Piece #4, #5
Cut 1—6" square
Cut square in half once
on the diagonal

Refer to General Instructions on pages 10-23 before beginning this block.

Watch Penny demonstrate the techniques used to make this block at landauerpub.com/Quilt-Block-Fusion-Penny-Haren.html.

CUTTING THE PAPER TEMPLATES

Cut one Template A on page 54.

Note: *The cutting instructions are optional. You may choose to paper-piece this block with scraps. However, if you are new to paper-piecing, cutting the fabric to the approximate size will make it easier. The finished block will also be more stable because the grain line of the fabric has been taken into consideration.*

Make one copy of the paper-piecing foundation on page 54. Do **not** include a seam allowance when cutting out the paper-piecing foundation.

PIECING

This block consists of 8 pieces.

1 Glue the A paper template to the wrong side of the bronze fabric triangle. Trim the fabric 1/4" away from the template on the straight sides. Trim the fabric approximately 1/4" away from the curved edges. Clip the inside curve. Turn both curved edges. These edges are marked with an "*".

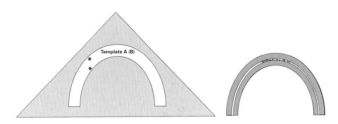

2 Sew a bronze #2A triangle to the left end of the light blue #2B rectangle. Press the seam open.

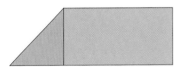

3 Sew a bronze #3A triangle to the right end of the light blue #3B rectangle. Press the seam open.

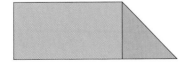

4 Paper-piece #1, #2A/2B, #3A/3B and #4 following Basic Paper-Piecing instructions on pages 12-16.

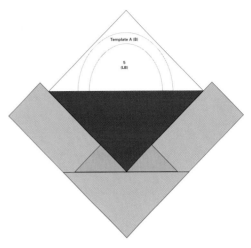

5 Center and glue the A appliqué on paper-piece #1, right sides together. The raw edges of the appliqué will be caught in the seam allowance when paper-piece #5 is added.

6 Paper-piece #5. Flip the A appliqué over paper-piece #5 and glue in position.

7 Trim the fabric 1/4" away from the paper-pieced foundation. Remove the foundation paper from the paper-pieced block.

8 Appliqué the handle in place. Follow the directions on page 23 to remove the paper template and glue.

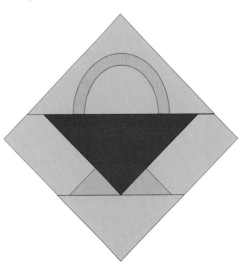

Templates & Foundation Blocks

RAMBLER

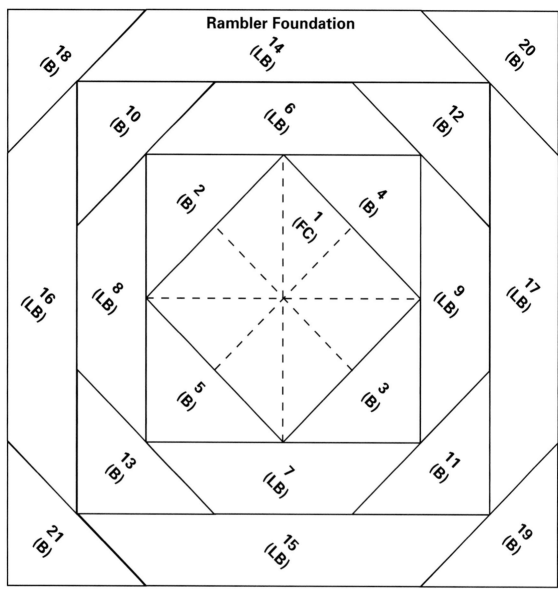

Rambler Foundation

18 (B)
14 (LB)
20 (B)
10 (B)
6 (LB)
12 (B)
2 (B)
1 (FC)
4 (B)
16 (LB)
8 (LB)
9 (LB)
17 (LB)
5 (B)
3 (B)
13 (B)
7 (LB)
11 (B)
21 (B)
15 (LB)
19 (B)

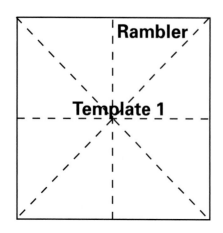

Rambler

Template 1

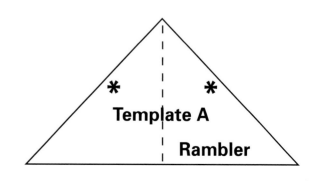

*   *

Template A

Rambler

CENTRAL PARK

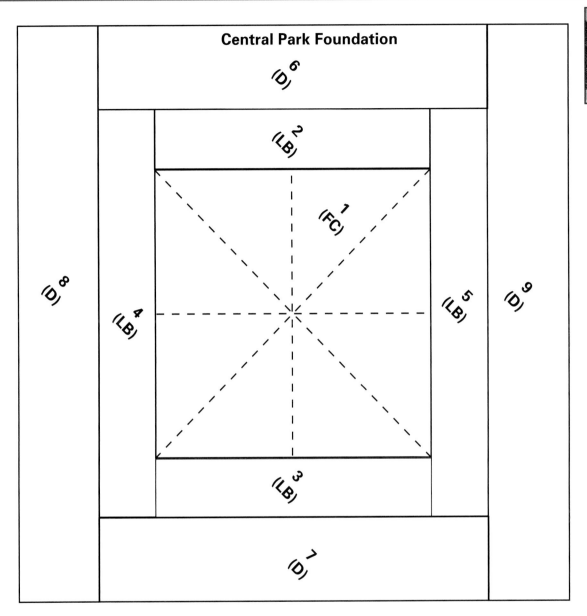

Central Park Foundation

6 (D)

2 (LB)

1 (FC)

8 (D)

4 (LB)

5 (LB)

9 (D)

3 (LB)

7 (D)

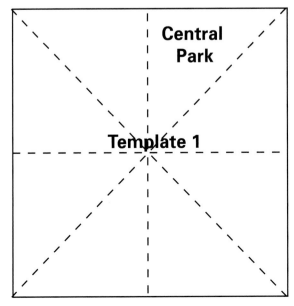

Central Park

Template 1

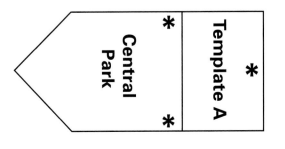

Template A

*

Central Park

*

*

POINTED DRESDEN PLATE

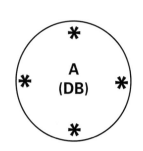

*
A
(DB)
*
*
*

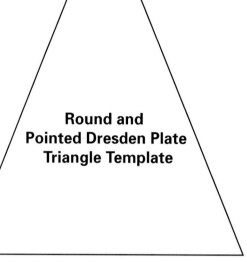

Round and Pointed Dresden Plate Triangle Template

Note: Use the Triangle Template if you are not using a 45˚ ruler to cut the Pointed and Round Dresden Plate triangles.

ROUND DRESDEN PLATE

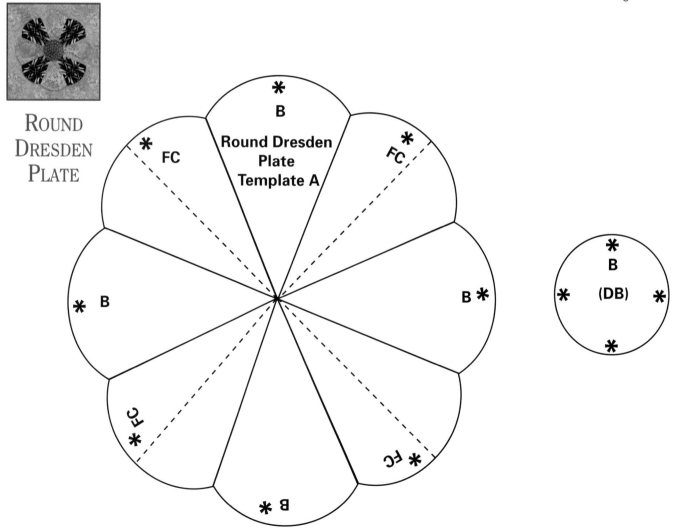

*
B
Round Dresden Plate Template A
*
FC
*
FC
*
B
*
B
*
FC
*
FC
*
B

*
B
(DB)
*
*
*

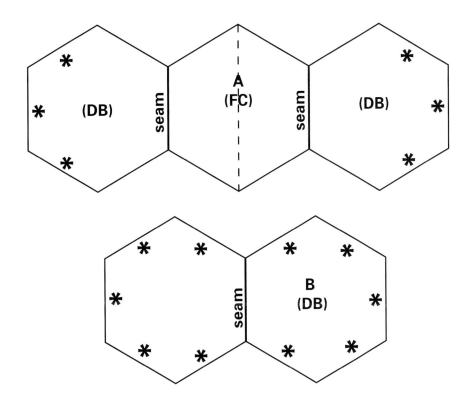

**STRIP-PIECED
GRANDMOTHER'S
FLOWER GARDEN**

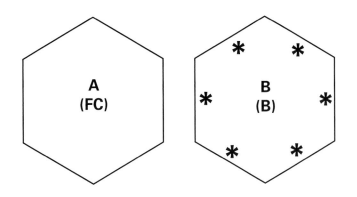

**MACHINE-PIECED
GRANDMOTHER'S
FLOWER GARDEN**

BASKET

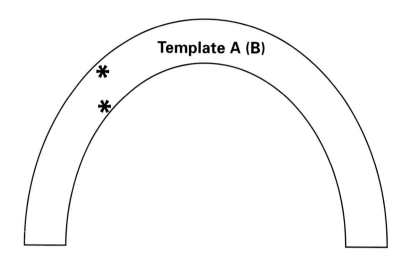

Template A (B)

*
*

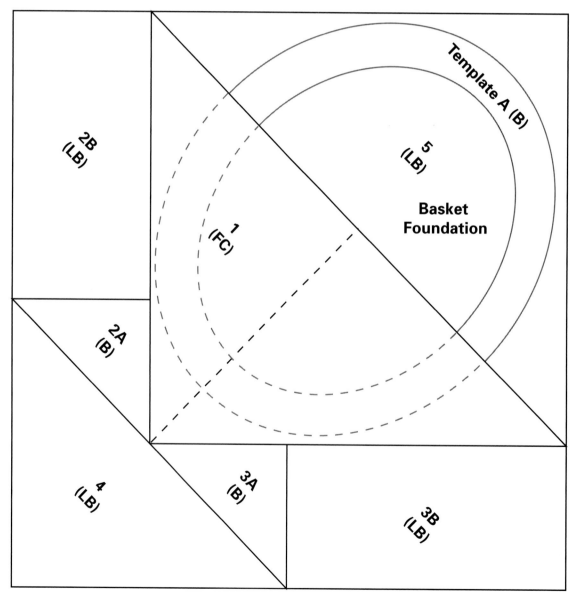

Template A (B)

2B
(LB)

5
(LB)

Basket
Foundation

1
(FC)

2A
(B)

4
(LB)

3A
(B)

3B
(LB)

Note: If you are making the Basket Table Topper on page 90, enlarge the basket template and foundation 150%.

Stars Over Tucson

Pieced by Helene Bednarczuk and Penny Haren; machine quilted by Cheryl Lorence

Finished Size: 75" Square

The Stars Over Tucson quilt is created with thirteen star blocks set on point. We chose to use each of the blocks taught in the book, but any six-inch block can be placed in the center of the star. Keep the final position of the fussy-cut fabric in mind if you are fussy-cutting your pieces.

Fabrics

All yardage requirements are based on 40"-wide, not pre-washed fabrics. Measurements include 1/4" seam allowance.

2 yards Fussy Cut Fabric
Note: *Yardage will vary depending on the repeat of your fabric. This yardage is based on a fabric with approximately a 5" repeat.*

1-3/4 yards Bronze Fabric

3/4 yard Light Blue Fabric

1-3/4 yards Ecru Fabric

1-1/4 yards Medium Blue Fabric

2-1/4 yards Black Dot Fabric

1/8 yard Dark Blue Fabric

4-1/2 yards of 40"- wide Backing Fabric or
2-1/4 yards of 90"-wide Backing Fabric

Machine-Pieced Grandmother's Flower Garden Block
Cutting
From the Fussy Cut Fabric:
    Use scraps to fussy cut 6 hexagons

From the Bronze Fabric:
    Use scraps to cut 1 hexagon

From the Ecru Fabric, cut:
    1—7" square
Paper Templates:
    Cut 6 Template A on page 53.
    Cut 1 Template B on page 53.

Strip-Pieced Grandmother's Flower Garden Block
Cutting
From the Fussy Cut Fabric, cut:
    1—2" strip, selvage to selvage

From the Ecru Fabric, cut:
    2—2-1/2" strips, selvage to selvage

Paper Templates:
    Cut 4 Template A on page 53.
    Cut 8 Template B on page 53.

Pointed Dresden Plate Block
Cutting
From the Fussy Cut Fabric, cut:
    1—2-3/4" strip, selvage to selvage

From the Bronze Fabric:
    1—2-3/4" strip, selvage to selvage

From the Dark Blue Fabric:
    Use scraps to cut 4 Appliqué A

Paper Templates:
    Cut 4 Template A on page 52.

Round Dresden Plate Block
Cutting
From the Fussy Cut Fabric, cut:
    1—2-3/4" strip, selvage to selvage

From the Bronze Fabric:
    1—2-3/4" strip, selvage to selvage

From the Dark Blue Fabric:
    Use scraps to cut 4 Appliqué B

Paper Templates:
    Cut 4 Template A on page 52.
    Cut 4 Template B on page 52.

Basket Block
Cutting
From the Fussy Cut Fabric:
    Paper-Piece #1
    Fussy cut 2—6" squares
    Cut once on the Diagonal

From the Bronze Fabric:
    Paper-Piece #2A, #3A
    Cut 2—4" squares
    Cut twice on the diagonal
    Cut 2—6" squares
    Cut once on the diagonal for Appliqué A

From the Light Blue Fabric:
    Paper-Piece #2B, #3B
    Cut 1—2-1/2" strip, selvage to selvage
    Sub cut the strip into
    8—2-1/2" x 4-1/2" rectangles
    Paper-Piece #4
    Cut 2—5" squares
    Cut once on the diagonal
    Paper-Piece #5
    Cut 2—6" squares
    Cut once on the diagonal

Paper Templates:
    Cut 4 Template A on page 54.

Fabrics Continued

Central Park Block

Cutting

From the Fussy Cut Fabric:
Paper-Piece #1
Fussy cut 4—4" squares

From the Bronze Fabric:
Appliqué A
Cut 1—2-1/2" strip, selvage to selvage

From the Light Blue Fabric:
Paper-Piece #2, #3, #4, #5
Cut 2—1-1/2" strips, selvage to selvage
Sub cut each strip into
4—1-1/2" x 4" rectangles for #2, #3 and
4—1-1/2" x 5-1/2" rectangles for #4, #5
Appliqué A
Cut 1—2" strip, selvage to selvage

From the Black Dot Fabric:
Paper-Piece #6, #7, #8, #9
Cut 4—2" strips, selvage to selvage
Sub cut each strip into
2—2" x 6" rectangles for #6, #7 and
4—2" x 7" rectangles for #8, #9

Paper Templates:
Cut 4 Template A on page 51.

Rambler Block

Cutting

From the Fussy Cut Fabric:
Paper-Piece #1
Fussy cut 4—3" squares

From the Bronze Fabric:
Paper-Piece #2, #3, #4, #5, #10, #11, #12,
#13, #18, #19, #20, #21
Cut 2—3" strips, selvage to selvage
Sub cut strips into
24—3" squares; cut once on the diagonal
Appliqué A
Cut 1—4" strip, selvage to selvage
Sub cut strips into 8—4" squares
Cut once on the diagonal

From the Light Blue Fabric:
Paper-Piece #6, #7, #8, #9, #14,
#15, #16, #17
Cut 4—2" strips, selvage to selvage
Sub cut each strip into
4—2" x 4" rectangles for #6, #7, #8, #9 and
4—2" x 6" rectangles for #14, #15, #16, #17

Paper Templates:
Cut 16 Template A on page 50.

Star Points

Cutting

From the Fussy Cut Fabric:
Paper-Piece #1
Fussy cut 52 squares using Star Point
Template A on page 66

From the Bronze Fabric:
Paper-Piece #4, #5
Cut 4—5" strips, selvage to selvage
Sub cut strips into 26—5" squares
Cut twice on the diagonal

From the Ecru Fabric:
Paper-Piece #2, #3
Cut 4—5" strips, selvage to selvage
Sub cut strips into 26—5" squares
Cut twice on the diagonal

Paper Templates:
Cut 52 Star Point Template A on page 66
if you are fussy cutting the star points.

Star Corners

Cutting

From the Fussy Cut Fabric:
Paper-Piece #1
Fussy cut 52 kite shapes using Star Corner
Template A on page 66

From the Ecru Fabric:
Paper-Piece #2, #3
Cut 6—4-1/2" strips, selvage to selvage
Sub cut strips into 52—4-1/2" squares
Using Template 2 on page 66, cut
26 of each with square right side up and
26 of each with square wrong side up

Paper Templates:
Cut 52 Star Corner Template A on page 66
if you are fussy cutting the star corners.

Setting Triangles, Corner Posts, Sashing, Border and Binding

Cutting

From the Bronze Fabric, cut:
2—3-1/2" strips, selvage to selvage
Sub cut strips into 12—3-1/2" squares
for corner post
3—6" squares, cut twice on the diagonal
for side setting corner posts

Making the Blocks

Machine-Pieced Grandmother's Flower Garden Block

Follow the Machine-Pieced Grandmother's Flower Garden Block technique notebook on page 33 to make one Grandmother's Flower Garden block on an ecru background.

Strip-Pieced Grandmother's Flower Garden Block

Follow the Strip-Pieced Grandmother's Flower Garden Block Piecing instructions on page 47 to make four Grandmother's Flower Garden blocks. The blocks will be appliquéd to the border later.

Round Dresden Plate Block

Follow the Round Dresden Plate Block instructions on page 39 to make four Round Dresden Plate blocks. The blocks will be appliquéd to the side setting triangles later.

Pointed Dresden Plate Block

Follow the Pointed Dresden Plate Block instructions on page 41 to make four Pointed Dresden Plate blocks. The blocks will be appliquéd to the side setting triangles later.

Basket Block

1 Make four copies of the paper-piecing foundation on page 54. Do not include a seam allowance when cutting it out.

2 Follow the Basket Block Piecing instructions on page 49 to make four Basket blocks.

Central Park Block

1 Make four copies of the paper-piecing foundation on page 51. Do not include a seam allowance when cutting it out.

2 Follow the Central Park Piecing instructions on page 37 to make four Central Park blocks.

Rambler Block

1 Make four copies of the paper-piecing foundation on page 50. Do not include a seam allowance when cutting it out.

2 Follow the Rambler Block Piecing instructions on page 35 to make four Rambler blocks.

MAKING THE STAR POINTS

1 Make 52 copies of the paper-piecing foundation on page 66 for the Star Points. Do not include a seam allowance when cutting them out.

2 Referring to Basic Paper-Piecing instructions on pages 12-16, paper-piece #1 through #5. Trim the fabric 1/4" away from the foundation paper on all sides. Remove the foundation paper.

3 Make 52 Star Points.

MAKING THE STAR CORNERS

Note: *Paper-pieces #2 and #3 for the Star Corners are odd shapes; therefore a template is provided. Glue two #2 templates to the fabric rectangle so the fabric extends at least 1/2" on all sides of the template. To cut four templates at once, two rectangles must be right side up and two must be wrong side up. Mirror images of the template can then be cut. Trim the fabric 1/2" away from the templates.*

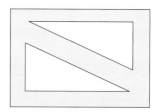

1 Make 52 copies of the paper-piecing foundation on page 66. Do not include a seam allowance when cutting them out.

2 Referring to Basic Paper-Piecing instructions on pages 12-16, paper-piece #1 through #3. Trim the fabric 1/4" away from the foundation paper on all sides. Remove the foundation paper.

3 Make 52 Star Corners.

PIECING THE STAR BLOCKS

1 Lay out the Machine-Pieced Grandmother's Flower Garden, four Star Points and four Star Corners, as shown.

2 Sew the pieces together in rows, pressing the seams open. Sew the rows together to make a Star Block.

3 Repeat steps 1-2 using the four Basket Blocks, four Central Blocks and four Rambler Blocks to make a total of 13 Star Blocks.

**Make 4
Basket Blocks**

**Make 4
Central Park Blocks**

**Make 4
Rambler Blocks**

APPLIQUÉING THE SIDE SETTING TRIANGLES

Note: *You may choose to appliqué the Dresden Plate Blocks to the side setting triangles after the quilt center is assembled.*

1 Center and appliqué four Pointed Dresden Plate Blocks on four ecru side setting triangles.

Note: *Since these triangles are over-sized, center the Dresden Plates based on the finished size of the triangles.*

2 Center and appliqué four Round Dresden Plate Blocks on four ecru side setting triangles.

3 There should be a total of eight appliquéd side setting triangles.

QUILT CENTER ASSEMBLY

1 Lay out the 13 Star Blocks, 36 medium blue sashing strips, 12 bronze corner posts, 12 bronze side setting corners posts, eight appliquéd side setting triangles and four corner triangles as shown in Quilt Assembly Diagram. The side setting triangles, side corner post triangles and corner triangles are over-sized.

2 Sew the pieces together in diagonal rows.

3 Sew the rows together to make the quilt center. Trim the over-sized triangles 1/4" beyond the points of the Star Blocks.

ADDING THE BORDERS

1 Sew the 8—6-1/2" black dot strips together on the diagonal to make one continuous strip.

2 Measure the length of the quilt top through the center. Cut two border strips to this measurement.

3 Sew these border strips to opposite sides of the quilt center. Press the seams toward the border strips.

4 Measure the width of the quilt top through the center. Cut two border strips to this measurement.

5 Sew these border strips to the top and bottom of the quilt center. Press the seams toward the border strips.

6 Center a Strip-Pieced Grandmother's Flower Garden Block to each border corner. Appliqué the block in place.

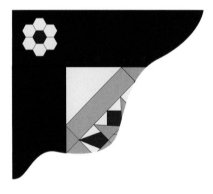

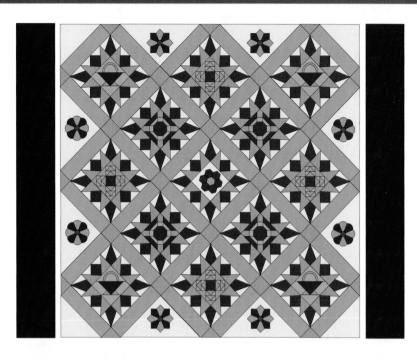

FINISHING THE PROJECT

1 Layer the top, batting and backing. Quilt as desired.

2 Sew the 2-1/4"-wide binding strips together on the diagonal to make one continuous strip.

3 Sew the binding to the quilt top, turn to the back and stitch in place.

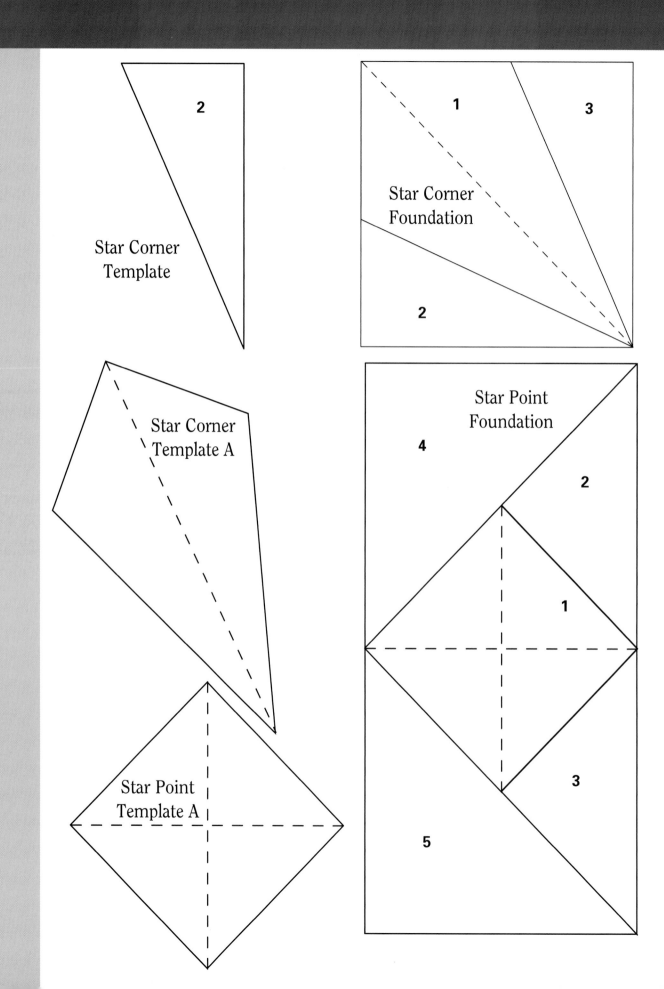

Star Corner Template

Star Corner Foundation

Star Corner Template A

Star Point Template A

Star Point Foundation

Stars Over Tucson
Finished Size: 75" Square

Pineapple Table Runner

Pieced by Ronice Kenny; machine quilted by Cheryl Lorence

Finished Size: 17-1/2" x 32-1/2"

This simple table runner is the perfect opportunity to practice your newly acquired paper-piecing skills. The Pineapple Block is a version of the Rambler Block without the pieced appliqué added. Fussy cutting adds additional interest to the block.

Fabrics

Note: All yardage requirements are based on 40"-wide, not pre-washed fabrics. Measurements include 1/4" seam allowance.

1 yard Stripe Fabric

> **Note:** *If fussy cutting, purchase additional fabric.*

3/4 yard Black Fabric

1/4 yard Ivory Fabric

3/4 yard Backing Fabric

3/4 yard Batting

Pineapple Block

Cutting

Note: The cutting instructions are optional. You may choose to paper-piece this block with scraps. However, if you are new to paper-piecing, cutting the fabric to the approximate size will make it easier. The finished block will also be more stable because the grain line of the fabric has been taken into consideration.

Stripe Fabric:
> Paper-Piece #1
> Fussy Cut 3—3" squares
> Paper-Piece #6, #7, #8, #9, #14, #15, #16, #17
> Cut 3—2" strips, selvage to selvage
> Sub Cut each strip into
> 4—2" x 4" rectangles (#6, #7, #8, #9) and
> 4—2" x 6" rectangles (#14, #15, #16, #17)

Note: *If you choose to fussy cut these units, center and cut each rectangle out of the same stripe.*

Black Fabric:
> Paper-Piece #2, #3, #4, #5, #10, #11, #12, #13, #18, #19, #20, #21
> Cut 18—3" squares
> Cut once on the diagonal

Borders and Sashing

Cutting

From the Ivory Fabric, cut:
> 4—2" x 6-1/2" rectangles for sashing units and inner borders
> 2—2" x 24-1/2" strips for inner borders

From the Black Fabric, cut:
> 2—1-1/2" x 9-1/2" units and
> 2—1-1/2" x 26-1/2" units for middle borders
> 4—3-1/2" squares for corner posts
> 3—2-1/4"-wide strips for binding

From the Stripe Fabric, fussy cut:
> 2—3-1/2" x 11-1/2" and
> 2—3-1/2" x 26-1/2" units for outer borders

Note: *If you choose to fussy cut the border units, center and cut each one out of an identical stripe.*

MAKING THE PINEAPPLE BLOCKS

Note: *The Pineapple Block is actually the Rambler Block without the pieced appliqué added.*

1 Make three copies of the Rambler paper-piecing foundation on page 50. Do not include a seam allowance when cutting them out.

2 Following the Basic Paper-Piecing instructions on pages 12-16, paper-piece #1 through #21.

Note: *If you choose to fussy cut the rectangles, extend the dashed line on the center square to the outside edges of the foundation. Center the rectangles on this line when paper-piecing.*

3 Trim the fabric 1/4" away from the foundation. Remove the foundation.

4 Make three Pineapple Blocks.

PUTTING IT ALL TOGETHER

Adding the Sashings and Inner Border

1 Sew a 2" x 6-1/2" sashing unit to opposite sides of one pineapple block. Sew a 2" x 6-1/2" sashing unit to one side of the two remaining Pineapple Blocks, as shown. Press the seams toward the sashing units.

 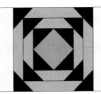 

2 Sew the 2" x 24-1/2" inner border to the top and bottom of the pieced unit in step 1. Press the seams toward the inner border.

Adding the Middle Borders

1 Sew a 1-1/2" x 9-1/2" middle border unit to opposite ends of the pieced center. Press the seams toward the middle border.

2 Sew a 1-1/2" x 26-1/2" middle border unit to the top and bottom of the pieced center. Press the seams toward the middle border.

Adding the Outer Border and Corner Posts

1 Sew a 2" x 11-1/2" outer border unit to opposite ends of the pieced center. Press the seams toward the outer borders.

2 Sew a 3-1/2"corner post to each end of the 3-1/2" x 26-1/2" outer border units. Press the seams toward the outer borders.

3 Sew the outer border units to the top and bottom of the pieced center. Press the seams toward the outer border.

FINISHING THE PROJECT

1 Layer the top, batting and backing. Quilt as desired.

2 Sew the 2-1/4"-wide binding strips together on the diagonal to make one continuous strip. Sew the binding to the quilt top, turn to the back and stitch in place.

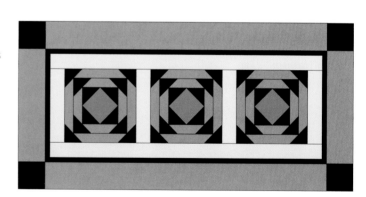

Pineapple Table Runner
Finished Size: 17-1/2 x 32-1/2" Square

Black Tie Affair Square

Pieced by Ronice Kenny; machine quilted by Cheryl Lorence

Finished Size: 36" Square

The Black Tie Affair wallhanging is constructed with a 6" block and paper-pieced star units. The Central Park Block was used in this project, but any block that finishes to 6" can be used. The star units are created in two different sizes to create this dramatic star within a star.

Fabrics

All yardage requirements are based on 40"-wide, not pre-washed fabrics. Measurements include 1/4" seam allowance.

Note: *You may wish to cut the Inner and Outer Star pieces first and then use the remaining fabric scraps to cut the Central Park Block pieces.*

1-1/4 yards White Stripe Fabric

3/4 yard Red Fabric

1-1/4 yards Black Fabric

2-1/4 yards Backing Fabric

42" x 42" Piece of Batting

Central Park Block

Cutting

Note: The cutting instructions are optional. You may choose to paper-piece this block with scraps. However, if you are new to paper-piecing, cutting the fabric to the approximate size will make it easier. The finished block will also be more stable because the grain line of the fabric has been taken into consideration.

Red Fabric:
Paper-Piece #1
Cut 1—4" square
Paper-Piece #6, #7, #8, #9
Cut 1—2" x 30" strip
Sub Cut the strip into
2—2" x 6" rectangles (#6, #7) and
2—2" x 7" rectangles (#8, #9)

Black Fabric:
Appliqué A
Cut 1—2-1/2" x 9" strip

White Stripe Fabric:
Paper-Piece #2, #3, #4, #5
Cut 1—1-1/2" strip, selvage to selvage
Sub Cut the strip into
2—1-1/2" x 4" rectangles (#2, #3) and
2—1-1/2" x 5-1/2" rectangles (#4, #5)
Appliqué A
Cut 1—2" x 9" strip

Paper Templates:
Cut 4 Template A on page 51.
The A appliqués will be pieced from the black fabric and white stripe fabric.

Star Units

Cutting
From the White Stripe Fabric, cut:
Inner Star
Paper-Piece #2, #3
Cut 2—6" squares
Cut twice on the diagonal
Outer Star
Paper-Piece #2, #3
Cut 2—12" squares
Cut twice on the diagonal
Inner Star Corner Units
Paper-Piece #1
Fussy cut 4 Kite Shapes using the Inner Star template on page 78. Trim the fabric 1/4" away from the templates on all sides.
Outer Star Corner Units
Paper-Piece #1
Fussy cut 4 Kite Shapes using the Outer Star templates on page 78. Trim the fabric 1/4" away from the templates on all sides.
Mitered Inner Border
Fussy cut 4—2" x 10" rectangles

From the Red Fabric, cut:
Inner Star
Paper-Piece #4, #5
Cut 4—6" squares
Cut once on the diagonal
Outer Star
Paper-Piece #4, #5
Cut 4—11" squares
Cut once on the diagonal

From the Black Fabric, cut:
Inner Star
Paper-Piece #1
Cut 4—4" squares
Outer Star
Paper-Piece #1
Cut 4—7" squares
Inner Star Corner Units
Paper-Piece #2, #3
Cut 4—4-1/2" x 5-1/2" rectangles
Outer Star Corner Units
Cut 4—9" x 12" rectangles
Binding
Cut 4—2-1/4"-wide strips

MAKING THE CENTRAL PARK BLOCK

1 Make one copy of the paper-piecing foundation on page 51. Do not include a seam allowance when cutting it out.

2 Follow the Central Park Block Piecing instructions on page 36 to make one Central Park block.

MAKING THE INNER STAR UNITS

1 Make four copies of the paper-piecing foundation on page 80 for the Inner Star Units. Do not include a seam allowance when cutting them out.

2 Referring to Basic Paper-Piecing instructions on pages 12-16, paper-piece #1 through #5. Trim the fabric 1/4" away from the foundation paper on all sides. Remove the foundation paper.

3 Make a total of 4—4-1/2" x 9" finished units.

MAKING THE OUTER STAR UNITS

1 Make four copies of the paper-piecing foundation on page 80, enlarging the templates 200 percent for the Outer Star Units. Do not include a seam allowance when cutting them out.

2 Referring to Basic Paper-Piecing instructions on pages 12-16, paper-piece #1 through #5. Trim the fabric 1/4" away from the foundation paper on all sides. Remove the foundation paper.

3 Make a total of 4—9" x 18" finished units.

MAKING THE INNER STAR CORNER UNITS

Note: Paper-pieces #2 and #3 for the Inner and Outer Star Corner Units are odd shapes; therefore a template is provided. Glue two #2 templates to the fabric rectangle so the fabric extends at least 1/2" on all sides of the template. To cut all four templates at once, two rectangles must be right side up and two must be wrong side up. Mirror images of the template can then be cut. Trim the fabric 1/2" away from the templates.

1   Make four copies of the paper-piecing foundation on page 79. Do not include a seam allowance when cutting them out.

2   Referring to Basic Paper-Piecing instructions on pages 12-16, paper-piece #1 through #3. Trim the fabric 1/4" away from the foundation paper on all sides. Remove the foundation paper.

3   Make a total of 4—4-1/2" finished units.

MAKING THE OUTER STAR CORNER UNITS

1   Make four copies of the paper-piecing foundation on page 79, enlarging the templates 200 percent for the Outer Star Corner Units. Do not include a seam allowance when cutting them out.

2   Referring to Basic Paper-Piecing instructions on pages 12-16, paper-piece #1 through #3. Trim the fabric 1/4" away from the foundation on all sides. Remove the foundation.

3   Make a total of 4—9" finished units.

PUTTING IT ALL TOGETHER

Piecing the Mitered Inner Border
Sew the white stripe 2" x 10" fussy-cut rectangles to the sides of the Central Park Block, mitering the corners. Press. The center block should now measure 9-1/2".

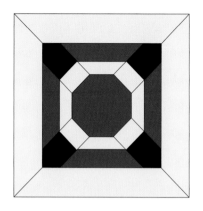

Piecing the Inner Star

1 Lay out the Central Park Block, four Inner Star Units and four Inner Star Corners, as shown.

2 Sew the pieces together in rows, pressing the seams open. Sew the rows together to make the Inner Star Block.

Piecing the Outer Star

1. Lay out the Inner Star Block, four Outer Star Units and four Outer Star Corners, as shown.

2. Sew the pieces together in rows, pressing the seams open. Sew the rows together.

FINISHING THE PROJECT

1. Layer the top, batting and backing. Quilt as desired.

2. Sew the 2-1/4"-wide binding strips together on the diagonal to make one continuous strip. Sew the binding to the quilt top, turn to the back and stitch in place.

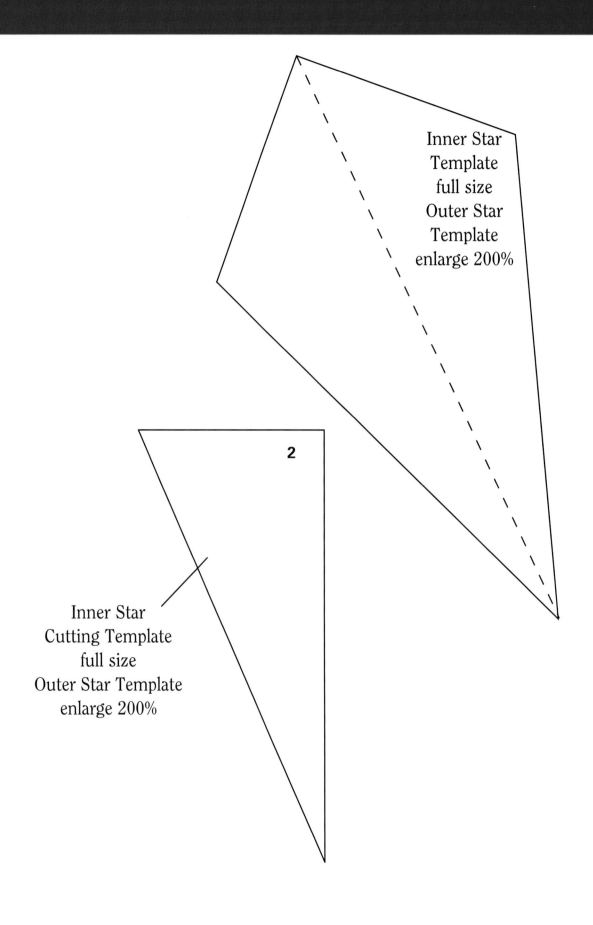

Inner Star
Template
full size
Outer Star
Template
enlarge 200%

2

Inner Star
Cutting Template
full size
Outer Star Template
enlarge 200%

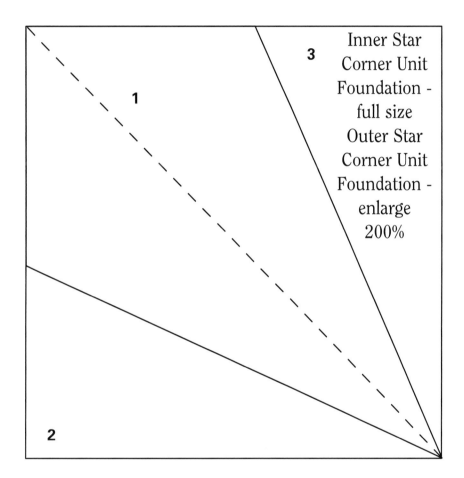

1

2

3 Inner Star
Corner Unit
Foundation -
full size
Outer Star
Corner Unit
Foundation -
enlarge
200%

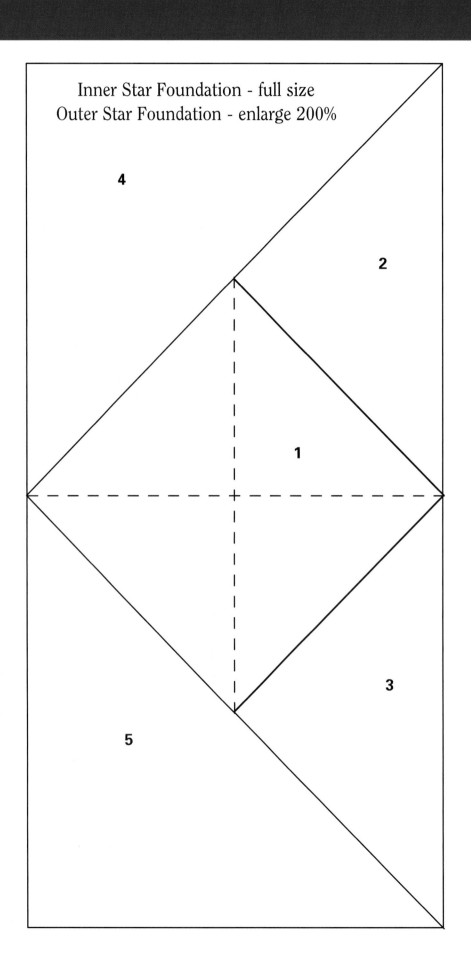

Inner Star Foundation - full size
Outer Star Foundation - enlarge 200%

Black Tie Affair
Finished Size: 36" Square

Pieced by Barb Campolo; machine quilted by Cheryl Lorence

Finished Size: 54-1/2" x 72-1/2"

Quick-to-make strip-pieced rows and Grandmother's Flower Garden blocks
make this quilt a fast and easy weekend project.

Fabrics

All yardage requirements are based on 40"-wide, not pre-washed fabrics. Measurements include 1/4" seam allowance.

1 fat quarter each of 14 different coordinating prints
(This quilt was made with scraps of reproduction fabrics. Some of the flowers will be duplicated.)

3/4 yard Green Print Fabric

1/8 yard Yellow Fabric

1-1/2 yards White Fabric

1/2 yard fabric for Binding

3-1/2 yards Backing fabric

2-1/4 yards 60"-wide Batting

Optional - Clover bias tape maker

Grandmother's Flower Garden Block

Our blocks were strip-pieced; see page 46. You may wish to machine-piece the blocks; see page 33.

Cutting

From each Fat Quarter, cut:
6—2-1/2" strips
> Sub cut 20 strips into 2—2-1/2" x 6" units and 2—2-1/2" x 3" units for the Grandmother's Flower Garden blocks
> The remaining 60 strips will be used for the strip-pieced rows

From the Green Fabric, cut:
1—27" square
> Sub cut the square into 3/4" strips to make 24' of 3/8" bias tape for vines.
> Note: The strips will stop and start at each flower, so piece the strips according to the length of vines you wish to have between flowers.
> The remaining green fabric will be used to cut the leaf appliqués

From the Yellow Fabric, cut:
1—3" strip
> Sub cut the strip into 20—2" x 3" units

From the White Fabric, cut:
8—6-1/2" strips, selvage to selvage

From the binding fabric, cut:
7—2-1/4" strips, selvage to selvage

Paper Templates, cut:
> 20 Strip-Pieced Grandmother's Flower Garden Template A on page 53
> 40 Strip-Pieced Grandmother's Flower Garden Template B on page 53
> 40 Leaf Templates on page 84

MAKING THE GRANDMOTHER'S FLOWER GARDEN BLOCKS

1 Follow the instructions on page 46 to construct the Grandmother's Flower Garden blocks. Make 20 Grandmother's Flower Garden blocks.
Note: If you prefer, use the templates on page 53 and follow the instructions on page 33 to machine-piece the blocks.

MAKING THE LEAF APPLIQUÉS

Glue the leaf paper templates to the wrong side of the remaining green fabric. Trim the fabric 1/4" away from the templates on all sides. Refer to page 21 to turn the fabric.

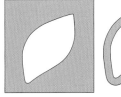 

MAKING THE STRIP-PIECED ROWS

1 Sew random sets of three fat quarter 2-1/2" strips together along the long edge. Press the seams to one side. Make 20 strip sets.

2 Cut each strip set into 3—6-1/2" squares.

3 Sew 12—6-1/2" squares together to make a strip-pieced row. Make five strip-pieced rows.

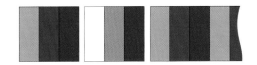

MAKING THE FLOWER ROWS

1. Remove the selvages from the 6-1/2" white fabric strips. Sew two strips together along the 6-1/2" edge to make a background row. Make four background rows.

2. Using the photograph on page 85 as a guide, lay out the bias vines, leaves and Grandmother's Flower Garden blocks on the four background rows. Allow room for the seam allowance in the background rows when placing the pieces.

Note: If you would like some of the flowers to stray into the strip-pieced rows, add these flowers after the rows have been sewn together.

3. Appliqué the pieces in place. Remove the paper templates and glue.

PUTTING IT ALL TOGETHER

1. Measure the strip-pieced rows and cut the flower rows to this length. The rows should measure 72-1/2".

2. Lay out the five strip-pieced rows and four flower rows as shown in the photograph on page 85.

3. Sew the rows together to complete the quilt top.

FINISHING THE QUILT

1. Layer the top, batting and backing. Quilt as desired.

2. Sew the 2-1/4"-wide binding strips together on the diagonal to make one continuous strip. Sew the binding to the quilt top, turn to the back and stitch in place.

Grandma Emma's Leaf Template

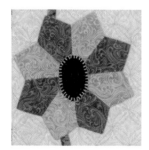

Design Option

Sunflower Dresden Plate Quilt

Replace the Grandmother's Flower Garden blocks with Pointed Dresden Plate blocks for a beautiful quilt for fall. The blocks are made in two shades of gold with an elongated center template and larger leaves.

Grandma Emma's Garden Quilt
Finished Size: 54-1/2" x 72-1/2"

Sydney's Quilt

Pieced by Jed Hanrahan

Finished Size approximately 44-1/2" x 58-1/2"

Round Dresden Plates in reproduction fabrics make a sweet quilt for a favorite grandchild.
The blocks go together quickly when using the pieced appliqué technique.

Fabrics

All yardage requirements are based on 40"-wide, not pre-washed fabrics. Measurements include 1/4" seam allowance.

1 fat quarter each of 8 different coordinating prints (purchase additional fat quarters for a scrappier look)

2-3/4 yards White Fabric

2/3 yard Purple Fabric

1/4 yard Yellow Fabric

1/2 yard Green Print Fabric

2-1/2 yards Backing Fabric

1-1/2 yards 90"-wide Batting or 50" x 65" Piece of batting

Round Dresden Plate Block

Cutting
From each Fat Quarter, cut:
    4—2-3/4" x width of fabric strips

From the White Fabric, cut:
    2—8" x length of fabric strips
        Sub cut the strips into
        24—8" background squares
    4—6-1/2" x length of fabric strips
    6—2-1/4"-wide strips for binding

From the Purple Fabric, cut:
    3—6-1/2" x width of fabric strips
        Sub cut the strips into
        58—2" x 6-1/2" sashing units

From the Yellow Fabric, cut:
    2—2" strips
        Sub cut the strips into 34—2" squares
Note: *Use the remaining yellow fabric scraps for the pieced appliqué centers of the Round Dresden Plate block.*

From the Green Fabric, cut:
    10—3/4" strips on the bias
Note: *Use the remaining green fabric for the leaf appliqués.*

Paper Templates, cut:
    34 Round Dresden Plate Template A on page 52
    34 Circle Template B on page 52
    20 Leaf Templates on page 88

MAKING THE ROUND DRESDEN PLATE BLOCKS

1 Follow the instructions on page 30 to construct the Round Dresden Plates using the 2-3/4" strips cut from the fat quarters and the yellow fabric scraps. Make 34 Round Dresden Plates.

2 Center a Round Dresden Plate on an 8" white background square. Appliqué in place. When the appliqué is complete, remove the templates and trim the finished block to 6-1/2". Make 24 Round Dresden Plate blocks.

PUTTING IT ALL TOGETHER

Piecing the Rows

1 Lay out five purple sashing units and four Round Dresden Plate blocks in a row, as shown.

2 Sew the pieces together to complete one block row. Make a total of six block rows. Press the seams toward the sashing units.

3 Lay out four purple sashing units and five 2" yellow squares in a row, as shown.

4 Sew the pieces together to complete one sashing row. Make a total of seven sashing rows. Press the seams toward the sashing units.

5 Lay out the seven sashing rows and six block rows as shown in the Quilt Center Diagram on page 88.

6 Sew the rows together to complete the quilt top. Press the seams toward the sashing rows.

ADDING THE BORDERS

1   Measure the length of the quilt top through the center. Cut a border strip to this measurement from each of the 6-1/2" white fabric strips.

2   Sew these border strips to opposite sides of the quilt center. Press the seams toward the border strips.

3   Measure the width of the quilt top through the center. Cut a border strip to this measurement from each of the 6-1/2" white fabric strips.

4   Sew these border strips to the top and bottom of the quilt center. Press the seams toward the border strips.

ADDING THE BORDER APPLIQUÉS

1   Make bias vines that finish 3/8"-wide from the 3/4" green fabric bias strips.

2   Glue the leaf templates to the wrong side of the green fabric. Trim the fabric 1/4" away from the templates on all sides and turn.

3   Using the photograph on page 89 as a guide, place the Dresden Plates, bias vines and leaves on quilt top borders. Appliqué the pieces in place.

FINISHING THE QUILT

1   Layer the top, batting and backing. Quilt as desired.

2   Sew the 2-1/4"-wide white binding strips together on the diagonal to make one continuous strip. Sew the binding to the quilt top, turn to the back and stitch in place.

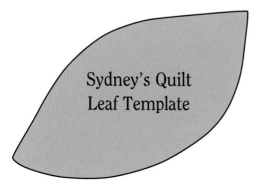

Sydney's Quilt
Leaf Template

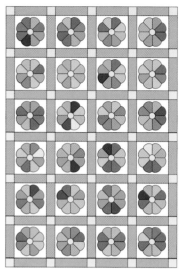

Quilt Center Diagram

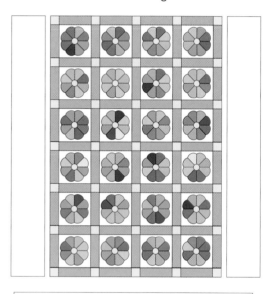

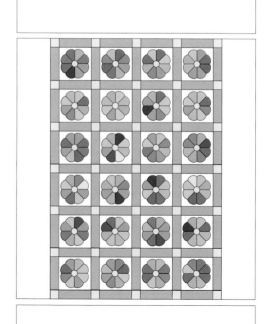

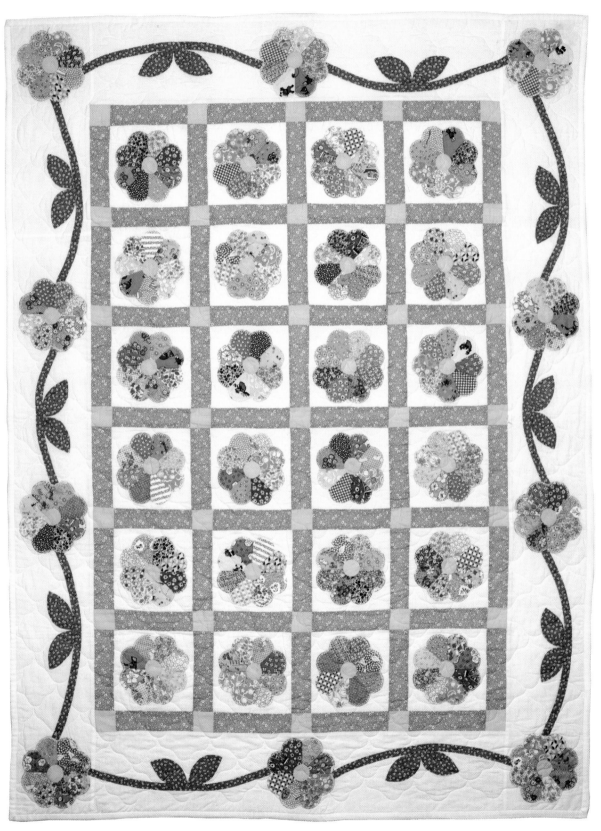

Sydney's Quilt
Finished Size: 44-1/2" x 58-1/2"

Basket Table Topper

Pieced by Landauer Staff; machine quilted by Cheryl Lorence

Finished Size approximately 27-1/2" x 27-1/2"

Create this eye-catching two color table topper with basket blocks and flying geese.

Fabrics

All yardage requirements are based on 40"-wide, not pre-washed fabrics. Measurements include 1/4" seam allowance.

1 yard Blue Fabric

1 yard White Fabric

1-3/4 yards Backing Fabric

33" x 33" Piece of Batting

Basket Block
Cutting

Note: The cutting instructions are optional. You may choose to paper-piece this block with scraps. However, if you are new to paper-piecing, cutting the fabric to the approximate size will make it easier. The finished block will also be more stable because the grain line of the fabric has been taken into consideration.

Blue Fabric:
Paper-Piece #1 and Handle
Cut 4—9" squares
Cut once on the diagonal
Paper-Piece #2A, #3A
Cut 4—4" squares
Cut once on the diagonal

White Fabric:
Paper-Piece #2B, #3B
Cut 8—3" x 6" rectangles
Paper-Piece #4
Cut 2—6" squares
Cut once on the diagonal
Paper-Piece #5
Cut 2—9" squares
Cut once on the diagonal

Flying Geese
Cutting
Blue Fabric:
Paper-Piece #1, #4, #7, #10, #13, #16
Cut 6—5" squares
Cut twice on the diagonal

White Fabric:
Paper-Piece #2, #3, #5, #6, #8, #9, #11, #12, #14, #15, #17, #18
Cut 24—3" squares
Cut once on the diagonal

Center, Borders and Binding
Cutting
Blue Fabric:
Cut 1—3-1/2" center square
Cut 4—1-3/4"-wide strips for outer border, selvage to selvage
Cut 3—2-1/4"-wide strips for binding

White Fabric:
Cut 4—2-1/2"-wide strips for inner border, selvage to selvage

Paper Templates:
Cut 4 Template A on page 54

MAKING THE BASKET BLOCK

1 Make four copies of the Basket paper-piecing foundation on page 54, enlarging it 150%. Do not include a seam allowance when cutting it out.

2 Follow the Basket block instructions on page 48 to make a total of four Basket blocks.

MAKING THE FLYING GEESE UNITS

1 Make four copies of the Flying Geese paper-piecing foundation on page 94. Do not include a seam allowance when cutting them out.

2 Referring to Basic Paper-Piecing instructions on pages 12-16, paper-piece #1 through #18. Trim the fabric 1/4" away from the foundation on all sides. Remove the foundation paper.

3 Make a total of 4 Flying Geese units.

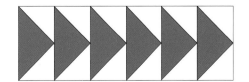

PUTTING IT ALL TOGETHER

Assembling the Table Topper Center

1 Lay out the 3-1/2" blue center square, four basket blocks and four flying geese units as shown.

2 Sew the pieces together in rows. Press the seams in each row in opposite directions.

3 Sew the rows together to make the table topper center.

Adding the Borders

1   Measure the table topper through the center. Cut two of the 2-1/2"-wide white inner border strips to this measurement. Sew to opposite sides of the table topper center. Press seams toward the borders.

2   Measure the table topper through the center, including the two added borders. Cut the remaining 2-1/2"-wide white inner border strips to this measurement. Sew to the remaining sides of the table topper center. Press seams toward the borders.

3   Measure the table topper through the center, including the outer border. Cut two of the 1-3/4"-wide blue outer border strips to this measurement. Sew to opposite sides of the table topper center. Press seams toward the borders.

4 Measure the table topper through the center, including the two added borders. Cut the remaining 1-3/4"-wide blue outer border strips to this measurement. Sew to the remaining sides of the table topper center. Press seams toward the borders.

FINISHING THE PROJECT

1 Layer the top, batting and backing. Quilt as desired.

2 Sew the 2-1/4"-wide binding strips together on the diagonal to make one continuous strip. Sew the binding to the quilt top, turn to the back and stitch in place.

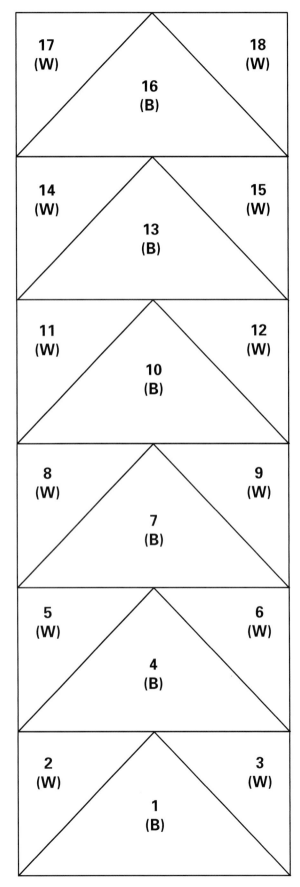

Basket Table Topper
Finished Size: 27-1/2" x 27-1/2"

Resources

Checker Distributors®
400 W. Dussel Drive, Suite B
Maumee, Ohio 43537-1636
(800) 537-1636
www.checkerdist.com

Creative Grids®
c/o Checker Distributors
400 W. Dussel Drive, Suite B
Maumee, Ohio 43537-1636
(800) 537-1636
www.creativegridsusa.com

Déjà vu by Paula Nadelstern
www.Benartex.com

**Simple Foundations Translucent
Velum Paper**
www.ctpub.com

C. Jenkins Freezer Paper Sheets
www.cjenkinscompany.com
(314) 521-7544

Acknowledgements

This book would not have been possible without "a little help from my friends". Their positive comments led to improvements in the techniques and markings on several occasions. So, thank you gals, I couldn't have done it without you.

Three ladies helped me sew samples and offered advice along the way, Helene Bednarczuk, Barb Campolo and Ronice Kenny. Thanks for all of the late nights—and in some cases, pajama parties so we could put this book to bed.

I am so fortunate that my "village" includes such generous, kind, and loving friends. Bless you all!

Love,
Penny